D0464577

UNDERSTANDING

ARNOLD WESKER

UNDERSTANDING CONTEMPORARY BRITISH LITERATURE

MATTHEW J. BRUCCOLI, *Editor*

Understanding Graham Greene
by R. H. Miller

Understanding Doris Lessing
by Jean Pickering

Understanding Arnold Wesker
by Robert Wilcher

UNDERSTANDING
Arnold
WESKER

by ROBERT WILCHER

UNIVERSITY OF SOUTH CAROLINA PRESS

Published in Columbia, South Carolina, by the
University of South Carolina Press

Manufactured in the United States of America

Library of Congress Cataloging-in-Publication Data

Wilcher, Robert, 1942—
   Understanding Arnold Wesker / by Robert Wilcher.
      p.   cm. — (Understanding contemporary British literature)
   Includes bibliographical references and index.
   ISBN 0–87249–760–7 (alk. paper)
   1. Wesker, Arnold, 1932–   —Criticism and interpretation.
I. Title.   II. Series.
PR6073.E75Z95   1991
822′.914—dc20   91–15703

To the Memory of Frank Norman Savage

CONTENTS

EDITOR'S PREFACE

Understanding Contemporary British Literature has been planned as a series of guides or companions for students as well as good nonacademic readers. The editor and publisher perceive a need for these volumes because much of the influential contemporary literature makes special demands. Uninitiated readers encounter difficulty in approaching works that depart from the traditional forms and techniques of prose and poetry. Literature relies on conventions, but the conventions keep evolving; new writers form their own conventions—which in time may become familiar. Put simply, *UCBL* provides instruction in how to read certain contemporary writers—identifying and explicating their material, themes, use of language, point of view, structures, symbolism, and responses to experience.

The word *understanding* in the series title was deliberately chosen. Many willing readers lack an adequate understanding of how contemporary literature works; that is, what the author is attempting to express and the means by which it is conveyed. Although the criticism and analysis in the series have been aimed at a level of general accessibility, these introductory volumes are meant to be applied in conjunction with the works they cover. Thus they do not provide a substitute for the works and authors they introduce, but rather prepare the reader for more profitable literary experiences.

M. J. B.

ACKNOWLEDGMENTS

Quotations from the following volumes are reproduced by permission of Penguin Books, Ltd.: *Arnold Wesker: Volume 1* (Penguin, 1979) (*Chicken Soup with Barley,* copyright Arnold Wesker, 1959, 1960; *Roots,* copyright Arnold Wesker, 1959, 1960; *I'm Talking about Jerusalem,* copyright Arnold Wesker, 1960, 1979); *Arnold Wesker: Volume 2* (Penguin, 1990) (*The Kitchen,* copyright Arnold Wesker 1960, 1961; *The Four Seasons,* copyright Arnold Wesker, 1966, 1990; *Their Very Own and Golden City,* copyright Arnold Wesker, 1966, 1981); *Arnold Wesker: Volume 3* (Penguin, 1980) (*Chips with Everything,* copyright Arnold Wesker, 1962; *The Friends,* copyright Arnold Wesker, 1970; *The Old Ones,* copyright Arnold Wesker, 1972, 1974); *Arnold Wesker: Volume 4* (Penguin, 1990) (*The Journalists,* copyright Arnold Wesker, 1975, 1990; *The Wedding Feast,* copyright Arnold Wesker, 1977, 1990; *Shylock* (formerly *The Merchant*), copyright Arnold Wesker, 1977, 1990); *Arnold Wesker: Volume 5* (Penguin, 1989) (*Whatever Happened to Betty Lemon?,* copyright Arnold Wesker, 1987; *Annie Wobbler,* copyright Arnold Wesker, 1987; *The Mistress,* copyright Arnold Wesker, 1989); *Arnold Wesker: Volume 6* (Penguin, 1990) (*Caritas,* copyright Arnold Wesker: 1981, 1990). I am grateful to Jonathan Cape, Ltd., for permission to quote from the following hardback editions of Wesker's works: *The Wesker Trilogy* (1960); *The Kitchen*

(1961); *Chips with Everything* (1962); *The Four Seasons* (1966); *Their Very Own and Golden City* (1966); *The Friends* (1970); *Fears of Fragmentation* (1970); *Six Sundays in January* (1971); *The Old Ones* (1973); *Love Letters on Blue Paper: Three Stories* (1974); *Said the Old Man to the Young Man: Three Stories* (1978); *The Journalists: A Tryptych* (1979); *Caritas* (1981); *Distinctions* (1985). Harper Collins Publishers has granted permission to quote from works in *The Plays of Arnold Wesker Volume I,* copyright © 1976 by Arnold Wesker (Harper & Row, 1976) (*The Kitchen, Chicken Soup with Barley, Roots, I'm Talking about Jerusalem,* and *Chips with Everything*) and in *The Plays of Arnold Wesker Volume II,* copyright © 1977 by Arnold Wesker (Harper & Row, 1977) (*Their Very Own and Golden City, The Friends,* and *The Old Ones*). Arnold Wesker has kindly permitted me to quote from the text of *Beorhtel's Hill* (1989), which was available from the Towngate Theatre, Basildon.

I am particularly grateful to Arnold Wesker for furnishing me with a list of recent publications and unpublished material and to Richard Lee, Head of Outreach and Play Officer at the Towngate Theatre, Basildon, for his prompt response to a request for a copy of the text of *Beorhtel's Hill* and for his generous supply of information about the 1989 production of the play.

More personal debts are owed to Sue Roberts and Jessica Wilcher for reading parts of the manuscript at an early stage, and to my wife, Miriam, and my younger daughters, Thomasin and Victoria, who endured the final stages of its preparation. Their support has been invaluable.

A NOTE ON TEXTS

Page references for all quotations from Wesker's plays are given in the text. Numbers in parentheses after quoted extracts refer to the Cape editions (where appropriate) and to the relevant volume of the Penguin collected edition. Thus (61; 3:179) indicates page 61 of the Cape edition of *The Old Ones* and page 179 of the Penguin *Arnold Wesker: Volume 3*. Page references for extracts from Wesker's prose works and for all other quotations are given in the notes.

UNDERSTANDING

ARNOLD WESKER

CHAPTER ONE

Life into Art

Arnold Wesker is a prolific and versatile writer. The author of more than thirty stage plays, he has also published collections of short stories and articles on a wide range of cultural and political topics. *Distinctions* (1985), which assembles many of his more fugitive pieces—essays, lectures, interviews, diaries, letters—contains three sections that reflect the breadth of his interests: one on various aspects of theater; one on such public issues as education, apartheid in South Africa, violence in Northern Ireland, Russian dissidents, the Falklands War of 1982, and the Palestinian problem; and one on the shortcomings of drama critics. The theatrical works for which he is best known will be the primary concern of this study, but it will draw upon the other writings to illuminate Wesker's themes and artistic practices.

Coming from a Jewish milieu "in which ideas were so important that their carriers were driven to actions which defined and changed their lives" (*Times Literary Supplement,* 3 May 1985), Wesker is best understood in the context of his often controversial views on and relation to society. For this reason, this book devotes a chapter to each of the four decades spanned by his career, with detailed discussions of plays that represent both the evolution of his theatrical craft and lines of continuity and development in his response to the public and private dimensions of human experience.

Career

Arnold Wesker was born in 1932 into an immigrant Jewish family in the East End of London, where his father was a garment worker. His formal education—at local infant and elementary schools and at Upton House Technical School in Hackney—came to an end when he was sixteen. Having failed to get a grant to take up a place at the Royal Academy of Dramatic Art, he became apprenticed to a furniture maker, on the principle that "I must take up a job, a trade, and if I was going to write I'd write anyway."[1] He moved on from one type of unskilled employment to another, first in London as a carpenter's mate, a bookshop assistant, and a plumber's mate, and then—after two years as a conscript in the Royal Air Force between 1950 and 1952—in Norfolk as a farm laborer, a seed sorter, and a kitchen porter. While working in Norwich, he met his wife, Dusty (Doreen) Bicker, who was a waitress in a hotel. He returned to London to train as a pastry cook in 1954 and later spent some months in a restaurant in Paris, where he saved enough money to enroll for a short course at the London School of Film Technique in 1956.

By this date, Wesker was already the author of poems, short stories, and an unpublished novel and had developed an ambition to be a film writer and director. His first theatrical work, *The Kitchen*, was written in response to a competition sponsored by a national Sunday newspaper in 1956; in the

2

same year, the English Stage Company's famous production of John Osborne's *Look Back in Anger* inspired him to write his second play, *Chicken Soup with Barley*. It was a meeting with the film director, Lindsay Anderson, that finally determined the direction Wesker was to take as an artist. Having approached Anderson about the possibility of filming one of Wesker's own short stories, Wesker also asked him to read the script of *Chicken Soup with Barley*. Anderson was impressed enough to recommend it to George Devine, artistic director of the English Stage Company, and the play was mounted at the Belgrade Theatre in Coventry, prior to a week's run at the Royal Court Theatre in London in July 1958. After *Roots* had also transferred from the Belgrade to the Royal Court and thence to a West End theater in the course of 1959, Wesker was hailed by one critic as "perhaps the most promising and mature of playwrights under thirty."[2] By the time *I'm Talking about Jerusalem* had been added in 1960 to complete what became known as the Wesker Trilogy and all three plays had been presented together at the Royal Court Theatre in the summer of that year, he was being described as "a major dramatist in the making."[3] *Chips with Everything* was voted Best Play of 1962 and in 1963 became the first of Wesker's works to be produced on Broadway.[4]

During the rest of the 1960s, however, much of Wesker's energy was diverted into the task of directing Centre 42, an ambitious project that aimed to make the arts more widely accessible to working-class communities. The British productions of his next three plays—*The Four Seasons* (1965), *Their Very Own and Golden City* (1966), and *The Friends* (1970)—received unfavorable notices, and his position in the London theater world was further damaged in 1972 by the acrimony

3

surrounding the withdrawal of *The Old Ones* from the scheduled program of the National Theatre and the row that led to the dramatist's filing a suit for breach of contract against the Royal Shakespeare Company over an abortive production of *The Journalists.* John Dexter, who had directed Wesker's first five plays, put *The Old Ones* on at the Royal Court Theatre later in 1972, but *The Journalists* had to wait until 1981 for its first professional production in Germany. Two earlier works had already had their premières in Brussels and Stockholm and the story of Wesker's later career was to be one of growing reputation overseas and comparative neglect at home. *The Wedding Feast* (1974), *The Merchant* (1976), *Love Letters on Blue Paper* (1977), and most of the short one-woman plays of the 1980s were first performed variously in Sweden, France, Japan, and the U.S. Subsequent productions in Britain, together with premières of *One More Ride on the Merry-go-round* (1985) and *When God Wanted a Son* (1989), have mostly been in provincial repertory theaters or in community or fringe theaters in the capital. Only *Love Letters on Blue Paper* in 1978 and *Caritas* in 1981 have been staged by the National Theatre Company. Interviewed in 1981, the playwright pointed out that three of his most important plays had never been produced on the London stage and commented, "If it weren't for the foreigners, I should be in despair."[5] *Lady Othello,* completed in 1987, had not yet been scheduled for production when it was published in 1990. Wesker's most recently performed new play, *Beorhtel's Hill* (1989), is a community drama written to celebrate the fortieth anniversary of Basildon, in Essex, one of the New Towns built after the Second World War.

4

Wesker's Dramatic Art: Themes and Methods

From the time the Trilogy first brought Arnold Wesker into the public consciousness, his achievements as a dramatist have been perceived in close relation to the details of his own life. An early review of *Chicken Soup with Barley* declared that "tolerance, enthusiasm, and warmth of heart are his message,"[6] and the more academic profiles that soon began to appear insisted on the connection between the man and the work. One influential assessment was prefaced with the remark that "it is virtually impossible to consider the plays apart from the playwright: to separate judgement of the plays as works of art from judgement of the political opinions."[7] The most comprehensive study of his work to date opens with the same point: "Of all modern dramatists Arnold Wesker must be one of the most—if not *the* most—personally involved in his own work."[8]

Wesker has frankly acknowledged that many of the characters and situations in his plays are taken directly from life. In the Trilogy, for example, Harry and Sarah Kahn "are—in so far as it is possible—total re-creations" of his own parents,[9] and "Beatie Bryant in *Roots* is the daughter of farm labourers in Norfolk, and my wife is the daughter of farm labourers in Norfolk."[10] *Chips with Everything* derived from a series of letters he wrote home during the eight weeks of his basic training in the RAF; and of *The Old Ones* he has said, "I'm full of admiration for all the relatives, aunts and uncles, who are mixed into that play."[11]

At the same time, however, Wesker has been careful to point out that "art is the re-creation of experience, not the

5

copying of it."[12] His usual method of composition is "to select and juxtapose and extend"[13] autobiographical material to serve purposes that go beyond the naturalistic portrayal of individuals and groups. Those purposes—and Wesker is the most purposeful of dramatists—have to do with the intellectual dimension of his experience, with those "political opinions" that cannot be ignored in any account of his evolution as an artist. They, too, like so many of his characters and situations, spring directly from the texture of his personal life, as he notes in an early article, "When I look back it seems to me that all my writings are attempts to resolve or continue more lucidly arguments I had with my family, my friends and the people with whom I worked."[14] The plays that followed the Trilogy have continued to emerge from and feed back into an ongoing debate about the function of art, both as a human phenomenon in the broadest terms and more specifically in the context of contemporary British society.

From the beginning, he has insisted that drama must be more than entertainment. "I want to teach," he announced in a youthful manifesto, entitled provocatively, "Let Battle Commence!" and went on to define art as "a tool" the artist places at the disposal of his audience, "equipment for the enjoyment of living, for its better understanding."[15] But if his plays have a didactic intention and are informed by a utopian vision that is socialist in orientation,[16] they do not offer a Marxist interpretation of history or elaborate a theory of political change. Kenneth Tynan was quick to recognize that Wesker's socialism was "more emotional than intellectual" and that the Trilogy revealed a dramatist who was "concerned less with economic analysis than with moral imperatives."[17] Always, at the heart of Wesker's dissatisfaction with capitalist society, there has been a conception of the good life that is fundamentally humanist in its emphasis. His first play puts on stage a powerful image of the dehumanizing effects of the daily routine in the kitchen of a large restaurant. It ends with the proprietor turning in bewilderment to his employees, after one of the cooks has gone berserk with a chopper and severed the pipe that supplies fuel to the ovens: "I give work, I pay well, yes? They eat what they want, don't they? I don't know what more to give a man. He works, he eats, I give him money. . . . What more do you want? What is there more, tell me? What is there more? What is there more? What is there more?" (78–79; 2:68–69).

Wesker believes that it is the artist's function to encourage people to find answers to that urgently reiterated question, and that as a socialist he has a particular responsibility toward those sections of the community in which, for historical reasons, "the desire to engage oneself, body and soul, in this wonderful process of living" has been stultified.[18] By the end of the 1950s, it seemed to the young writer from the East End that the political advances made by the labor movement over the previous century and a half, culminating in the establishment of the Welfare State by the postwar Attlee government, had opened the way for the working classes to look beyond the narrow horizons imposed by the need for mere economic survival, "It is now possible—because of the economic advantages gained by the unions and the socialist Parties—for everyone to read books from the libraries, listen to concerts on the radio, visit the theatres and in general take part in the cultural life of the community."[19] As one of the generation of dramatists beginning to break into a theatrical world that had long been the preserve of the socially privileged, his ambition

7

was to make contact with a new audience: "I want to write my plays not only for the class of people who acknowledge plays to be a legitimate form of expression, but for those to whom the phrase 'form of expression' may mean nothing whatsoever. It is the bus driver, the housewife, the miner and the Teddy Boy to whom I should like to address myself."[20]

Wesker recognized from the outset, however, both that the alienation of this potential audience from mainstream culture was deeply rooted in historical circumstances and that it would take more than wishful thinking or impassioned speeches in plays performed at London's Royal Court Theatre to change the intellectual habits of an entire social class. Having come to the conclusion that "rebellious words are not enough,"[21] he launched a one-man campaign to mobilize the resources of the Left in support of his vision. In a lecture given to the participants in a Student Drama Festival in Oxford in the spring of 1960, the text of which was later distributed to the general secretaries of every trade union in the country, he indicted the Labour movement for "a neglect which I consider almost immoral" in ignoring the fact that socialism is "not merely an economic organization of society but a way of living based on the assumption that life is rich, rewarding and that human beings deserve it."[22] In a subsequent pamphlet, he listed several practical projects and suggested that the unions should set up an independent inquiry into the state of the arts. Because of this effort, a resolution was placed before the Trades Union Congress by the Association of Cinematograph, Television and Allied Technicians in September 1960, which called upon delegates to recognize "the importance of the arts in the life of the community, especially now when many unions are securing a shorter working week and greater leisure for their members'' and concluded with a request to the General Council ''to conduct a special examination and to make proposals to a future Congress to ensure a greater participation by the trade union movement in all cultural activities.''[23] Against the advice of the General Council, this resolution—number forty-two on the agenda—was unanimously passed, and over the next few months Wesker and a group of like-minded artists evolved the concept of Centre 42. Wesker himself was elected onto the first provisional steering committee and eventually agreed to take on the role of artistic director of the project. The socialist values shared by the members of the group were enunciated in the report of the first committee meeting, ''These values imply for us the necessity of shifting all emphasis from the monetary and competitive values of life, which tend to isolate man from man, to those values which reaffirm the sense of community, and thereby a sense of responsibility that all men should have for each other.'' Their primary objective, as it was set out in the *Annual Report 1961–1962,* was the founding of an arts center to serve as ''a cultural hub,'' which, by its approach and work, would ''destroy the mystique and snobbery associated with the arts'' and, by bringing artists into closer contact with their audiences, would enable the public ''to see that artistic activity is a natural part of their daily lives.'' The center, which was to be the prototype for others, would not only serve its immediate locality but also constitute a reservoir of talent and material to be drawn upon by community bodies elsewhere. While the plans for such a center were still being discussed, an invitation from the Trades Council in Wellingborough resulted in a fourday festival of drama, painting, poetry, and music in 1961.

The success of this first venture led to the mounting of five more arts festivals in various parts of the country during 1962.

Despite the impact of these festivals on the cultural scene in Britain, the Council of Fortytwo decided not to accept further invitations until they had secured a suitable base for their artistic and administrative activities. It was not until 1964 that Wesker finally acquired the lease of a Victorian engine shed in the Chalk Farm district of London and engaged an architect to draw up plans for its conversion into a permanent home for Centre 42. Unable to raise sufficient funds to adapt the Round House into the kind of community arts center he had originally envisaged, Wesker was forced to accept an interim scheme to develop the building as a performing space that other people could hire. He became disenchanted with what was now merely a commercial enterprise, and his decision to resign from the artistic directorship led to the official dissolution of Centre 42 in December 1970.[24]

The cultural project to which Wesker had devoted ten years of his life—"to make the pursuit of the extraordinary experience of art an unextraordinary pursuit"[25]—had ended in defeat, and not for the first time in his career, the conflict between idealism and the harsh facts of reality provided the thematic material for drama. The Trilogy, with its long time-span from 1936 to 1959, had charted the gradual fading of Communist faith and youthful energy among a group of Jews in the East End of London, as the buoyant optimism generated by the struggle against Oswald Mosley's fascists during the 1930s had been eroded by the grip of postwar Stalinism on the countries of Eastern Europe and the election of three successive Conservative governments in Britain during the

1950s. The two plays that came directly out of Wesker's experiences with Centre 42, *Their Very Own and Golden City* and *The Friends,* explore the failure of the dreams of his own generation. But, although Wesker has frequently dealt with the theme of disappointed hopes and unfulfilled ambitions, his is far from being a theater of despair. His idealism has always been tempered by a realistic acknowledgment of the magnitude of the problems that confront revolutionary and reformer alike, and he has been careful to avoid the ''great trap'' of formulating ''universal philosophies out of our personal failures and unhappiness.''[26] Time and again, he has dramatized not only the collapse of idealistic projects but also the resilience of the human spirit that keeps idealism alive in the midst of defeat. For example, while her companions give way to despair and self-pity, Esther, dying of leukemia during the first act of *The Friends,* celebrates the joy of being alive and the ever-renewed hope for the future: ''Every year the world finds something new to offer me: another man makes music or carves an impossible shape out of the rocks or sings us a poem. Someone is always rising up, taking wing, and behind him he pulls the rest of us; and I want to be there, for every movement, every sound'' (32; 3:94). After her death, Simone, the most self-effacing member of the group, slowly grows in confidence and emerges by the end of act 2 as the true inheritor of Esther's vision and spirit. The same thematic pattern occurs in *The Merchant,* as the tired and defeated Shylock hands on his enthusiasm for life and his respect for learning to Portia, his spiritual daughter.

Another recurrent theme, which is closely associated with the Centre 42 project and which reflects a latent contradiction in Wesker's dual commitment to socialism and humanism, is

11

that of the community and the individual. In act 3 of *Chicken Soup with Barley,* a middle-aged Monty looks back nostalgically to the sense of communal purpose that united the young "comrades" of act 1. Early in the final play of the Trilogy, Sarah Kahn identifies the political flaw in her son-in-law's plan to opt out of the competitive society and restore the dignity of his own labor by fashioning handmade furniture in an isolated workshop in the countryside: "The city is human beings. What's socialism without human beings tell me?" (166; 1:164).

But while Wesker has always recognized the need for collective action to bring about a more just and vibrant society, he has never denied the claims of the individual. *The Four Seasons* marked a significant change of direction in his dramatic approach, with its exclusive focus on the intimate sexual and emotional relationship between one man and one woman. Hitherto, he had portrayed human beings as members of a social class or a hierarchical organization, defined primarily by their place in a political and economic structure—as the exploited cosmopolitan workforce in a large kitchen, as agricultural laborers, as conscripts in the RAF. It is noteworthy that he felt compelled to add an epilogue to the Penguin edition of the play (1966), justifying this development in his art:

> There is an argument which says that individual or private pain can have no relevance in a society where man's real tragedies are bound inextricably with his social environment; a story unrelated to and ignoring social and political events is a story that has no truth or validity. To which I make this reply: If compassion and teaching the possibility of change are two of the many effects of art, a third is

this: to remind and reassure people that they are not alone not only in their attempts to make a better world but in their private pains and confusions also. . . . There is no abandoning in this play of concern for socialist principles nor a turning away from a preoccupation with real human problems; on the contrary, the play, far from being a retreat from values contained in my early writing, is a logical extension of them. (2:113–14)

The tensions evident in this polemical defense of his artistic practice were later to become open doubts about the nature of contemporary socialism. Challenged by an interviewer to define his political position in 1977, he confessed, "It seems to me that what I've always been is a simple, old-fashioned humanist":

You see, while I'd like to think that I've lost none of my capacity for outrage against inequality and injustice, yet I suppose I'm increasingly worried about contributing towards the creation of a state of society which then considers it is doing me a favour in giving me my liberty. . . . I think there are a lot of people who still feel that we are the socialists we always were, but that somehow we are out on a limb, floating in space, drawing inspiration from no one political movement, but from a long history of . . . what? Rationalist action? Humanist philosophy?[27]

Wesker did not abandon public themes in the plays that followed *The Four Seasons,* but he increasingly emphasized the "private pains and confusions" associated with loneliness and the approach of death and the courage with which characters like Teressa in *The Old Ones* and Betty Lemon cope with the isolation and physical handicaps that come with old age. There was also a growing sense of the "inspiration" to be drawn from the "long history" of humanist thought and from what he called elsewhere "twenty centuries of man's accumulated sensibilities and experience."[28] As Simone puts it in *The Friends,* "The past is too rich with human suffering and achievement to be dismissed" (69; 3:124). Soon after writing that play, Wesker, who had once denied that he regarded himself as a specifically Jewish playwright, admitted that he had recently begun to feel more "protective" about his Jewish origins, "I think that what happens is that you are suddenly aware that you have inherited a shared consciousness of your community's suffering."[29] In *The Merchant* (which Wesker has since retitled *Shylock*), he rewrites Shakespeare's version of the story of Antonio and Shylock in the light of research into the history of the Venetian ghetto in the sixteenth century and his own understanding of Jewish culture and values. By 1982, he was seeking to identify "the nature of Jewishness as I believe it pervades my work."[30]

During the same interview in which he spoke of a growing awareness of his Jewish heritage, Wesker pointed out the common concern that links a play like *Roots* to the Centre 42 project and traced it back to "a kind of intense fear of brutishness . . . a fear inherited from the community."[31] That fear—of the mindless violence that can so easily erupt when human beings have no other means of expressing the frustrations of their lives—manifests itself in such dramatic images as the violent severing of the gas pipe at the end of *The Kitchen;* and that concern—with the dissemination of civilized values through the medium of art—manifests itself in many of the plays as a preoccupation with the need to respect language. When Beatie Bryant recalls Ronnie's belief that words are "bridges, so that you can get safely from one place to another" (88; 1:90) and Shylock lectures the Venetians on the Gutenberg revolution and the revival of learning after the Dark Ages—"The word! Unsuspected! Written! Printed! Indestructible!" (4:229)—they are part of a thread that runs through all Wesker's work and connects his early declaration of war on "the facile, blind arguments, the platitudinous phrases which are the barricades of the man in the street to anything new" with a much later pamphlet in which he spells out the connection between his humanism and his political orientation: "To me, as a Socialist, if education means anything it means essentially this: the upholding of language as man's greatest creation. It means a constant freshening, a constant guarding against abuse by demagogues, bureaucrats and copy-writers, whether political or commercial."[32]

Wesker has not only explored the theme of language as an essential tool for living, but as a dramatist he has also been concerned with the nature and function of language on the stage. His first four plays earned him the label of "social realist"; and critics have written approvingly of his mastery of the Jewish verbal rhythms of his East Enders and the Norfolk dialect of the Bryant family in *Roots,* the "warm, lived in, believable quality which is characteristic of Wesker's dialogue at its best."[33] Gareth Lloyd Evans agrees, "Few dramatists in the history of drama in this country have used dialect as convincingly as does Wesker in his Trilogy," but considers that his most significant achievement "was to dissociate dialect from inferiority, and to give it a valid currency for expression."[34] This is high praise, but it carries with it a damaging corollary that has dogged Wesker ever since he experimented with the stylized naturalism of *Chips with Everything* and the lyricism of *The Four Seasons.* Lloyd Evans's verdict is that "the language of the later plays embroiders rather than embodies" the undiminished passion of Wesker's commitment to the quality of human existence, and that, even in the early Trilogy, he "showed a tendency to abandon the directness of straight prose-speech whenever he wished to express an 'inner' mood, compulsion, attitude, enthusiasm, emotion."[35] Wesker himself, while recognizing "the trap of creating a pseudo-poetic dialogue," defended the style of *The Four Seasons* as a necessary step in his personal development as an artist: "The words and rhythms of everyday speech are rich and contain their own poetry, but after a time they cease to be adequate. In six plays . . . I had wrung from such speech rhythms all that I was able, at least for the moment, and wanted to create a heightened and lyrical language" (2:112–13). Elsewhere, he has justified both the disruption of predominantly naturalistic stretches of dialogue by rhetorical or poetic passages and the staging of discussion, "people scoring points on each other intellectually or even opening out their hearts—being impassioned—this is for me drama."[36] In a talk in 1985, he developed further his view that even the most realistic speech in the theater is a result of selection not direct transcription, and that "the texture of the dialogue" in any particular play "is dictated by the material."[37]

In spite of this highlighting of the function of language in life and theater, Wesker's dramatic methods have always exhibited a strong "pull towards the physical," which, in such works as *Chips with Everything,* threatens "to turn his drama expressionistic."[38] During the process of writing that play, he spoke of his conscious movement away from naturalistic scenery and dialogue as he became "aware more and more that the theatre is a place where one wants to *see* things happening."[39] His plays are full of the everyday actions that occupy so much of people's lives: the routines of work in the kitchen of a city restaurant or the offices of a national newspaper; the daily chores of cooking and cleaning in a farm laborer's cottage; the social rituals of bathing and dressing, eating and drinking. Sometimes, in *The Kitchen* or *The Journalists,* he orchestrates the complex interaction of large numbers of people pursuing a common end, so that "one gets a real sense of work rhythms: of physical activity striving to fill—and fulfil—space."[40] Sometimes, he focusses attention sharply on the skilled performance of an individual act, the deft dismembering of an orange in *Love Letters on Blue Paper* or the preparation of an apple strudel in *The Four Seasons.*

The theatrical dynamic—now dispersing attention over business that utilizes every corner of the stage and now concentrating it upon an isolated and technically demanding feat by a single actor—is just one aspect of a dramaturgy that exploits the tension between opposites in a variety of ways. It is a failure to respond to this feature of his art that has led to repeated charges that the plays are poorly constructed and unsubtle in their preaching of rigidly formulated messages.[41] For all his declared didactic purpose, Wesker creates dramatic contexts for the exposition of his ideas that allow full scope for countercurrents of argument and emotion. The audience's reception of the intellectual content of a speech is likely to be complicated by the personality or situation of the speaker, and the content may itself be challenged explicitly by other speakers as the drama unfolds. Above all, the competing claims of the individual and the wider society and the contradictory impulses of hope and despair inform both the thematic substance and the formal lineaments of play after play. Peter Bowering has commented on "the polarities of Wesker's drama," which turn it into "an extended debate on whether optimism or pessimism is the natural state of man"; and the playwright himself has described the structure of the Trilogy and *Their Very Own and Golden City* as deliberately designed to satisfy "that part of me which wants to encourage an energy based on hope tempered by the knowledge of the pessimistic possibilities."[42] For his analysis of the complex intellectual and emotional issues raised by the collapse of Centre 42 in *The Friends,* Wesker created what Michael Kustow has called "a self-balancing yet restless dramatic structure which puts a question-mark against every apparently final assertion." Since then, he has gone on to perfect "a constructional principle" that Kustow compares variously to that of a mobile, a collage, and a kaleidoscope. Details are juxtaposed, fluctuate, collide, yet continually "settle into a recognizable order, incorporating even the most refractory elements."[43]

Arnold Wesker regards himself as the victim of "what is known as 'the frozen image.' " He elaborated on this concept in a paper to the biennial conference of the International Association of Theatre Critics in Rome in 1985: "My image appears to be that of what is crudely known as a 'socially realistic' playwright. It's a description I've had to fight off for 27 years and one I've always resented, because it has blinded people to those other elements in my work which I'd always hoped would be recognized: the paradoxical, the lyrical, the absurd, the ironic, the musical, the farcical, etc."[44] This bias is certainly borne out by the conclusions of a recent study of postwar British drama: "Despite a continuing, courageous concern for the primacy of humane values and their exploration in drama, Wesker has never again been able to express this preoccupation with the force of the *Trilogy;* the same questions recur but the dramatic answers become more elusive."[45] It is the purpose of the ensuing chapters to challenge this judgment on the later plays, and, while directing attention to the recurrent themes which witness to the continuity of the "rational vision"[46] that has sustained Wesker throughout his career, to argue that his development as a theatrical craftsman is also worthy of close and serious scrutiny.

NOTES

1. Simon Trussler, "His Very Own and Golden City," 80.

2. Laurence Kitchin, "Playwright to Watch," 195.

3. Richard Findlater, "Plays and Politics," 236.

4. *Roots* had already appeared in an Off-Broadway production at the Mayfair Theater in 1961.

5. Maureen Cleave, "If it weren't for the foreigners, I should be in despair," 35.

6. Review by John Arden in *Encore* 5 (September-October 1958); reprinted in *The Encore Reader,* ed. Charles Marowitz, Tom Milne, and Owen Hale (London: Methuen, 1965), 92.

7. John Russell Taylor, *Anger and After: A Guide to the New British Drama,* 147.

8. Glenda Leeming, *Wesker the Playwright,* 1.

9. Ronald Hayman, "First Interview," in *Arnold Wesker,* 2.

10. Trussler, "His Very Own and Golden City," 79.

11. Simon Trussler, Catherine Itzin, and Glenda Leeming, "A Sense of What Should Follow," 11.

12. Wesker, "Discovery," 17.

13. Trussler, "His Very Own and Golden City," 79.

14. Wesker, "Discovery," 16.

15. Wesker, "Let Battle Commence!" 96, 98.

16. Wesker records that he was "a member of the Young Communist League for a short while" in Trussler, "His Very Own and Golden City," 80.

17. Review of *Chicken Soup with Barley* (1960); reprinted in Kenneth Tynan, *A View of the English Stage*, 291.

18. Wesker, "O Mother Is It Worth It?" (April 1960); reprinted in *Fears of Fragmentation*, 15.

19. Ibid., 16.

20. Wesker, "Let Battle Commence!" 96.

21. Wesker, "The Secret Reins" (March 1962); reprinted in *Fears of Fragmentation*, 45.

22. Wesker, "O Mother Is It Worth It?"; reprinted in *Fears of Fragmentation*, 17.

23. Quoted by Frank Coppieters, "Arnold Wesker's Centre Fortytwo: A Cultural Revolution Betrayed," 39. The quotations in the rest of the paragraph are from documents cited by Coppieters.

24. The report on Wesker's proposals, delivered to the 1961 Congress and promptly shelved, had declared that cultural affairs were not the concern of trades unions. No money was allocated to the project by the TUC, although several union leaders were on the provisional council of Centre 42 in its early days. In 1965, in response to an appeal for funds, Wesker was informed that the General Council felt no responsibility toward the project.

25. Wesker, "The Allio Brief" (August 1964); reprinted in *Fears of Fragmentation*, 52.

26. Wesker, "Theatre, Why?" (June 1967); reprinted in *Fears of Fragmentation*, 87.

27. Trussler, Itzin, and Leeming, "A Sense of What Should Follow," 20.

28. Wesker, "Theatre, Why?"; reprinted in *Fears of Fragmentation*, 96.

29. Hayman, "First Interview," in *Arnold Wesker*, 5. It was in an interview in New York in 1964 that Wesker declared himself to be Jewish and a playwright, rather than a Jewish playwright. See Walter Wager, ed., *The Playwrights Speak*, 220.

30. Wesker, "The Two Roots of Judaism" (November-December 1982); reprinted in *Distinctions*, 252.

31. Hayman, "First Interview," in *Arnold Wesker*, 4.

32. Wesker, "Let Battle Commence!" 101; Wesker, *Words as Definitions of Experience*, 4.

33. Katharine J. Worth, *Revolutions in Modern English Drama*, 21.

34. Gareth Lloyd Evans, *The Language of Modern Drama,* 90–91.

35. Ibid., 89, 96.

36. Hayman, "Second Interview," in *Arnold Wesker,* 93, 98.

37. Wesker, "The Nature of Theatre Dialogue," 364.

38. Worth, *Revolutions,* 30, 35.

39. Wesker, "Art is Not Enough," 192.

40. Richard Appignanesi, "Finding One's Own Voice: An Afterword on Wesker's WORDS and His Plays," 32.

41. See, for example, Taylor's comments on ideas "inartistically crammed in as sermons delivered by the playwright's mouthpiece" and "Wesker's casualness about construction" in *Anger and After,* 147, 157.

42. Peter Bowering, "Wesker's Quest for Values," 71; Hayman, "First Interview," in *Arnold Wesker,* 10–11.

43. Michael Kustow, "Wesker at the Half-way House," 33.

44. Wesker, "The Nature of Theatre Dialogue," 366–67.

45. Colin Chambers and Mike Prior, *Playwrights' Progress: Patterns of Postwar British Drama,* 145.

46. The phrase is Appignanesi's in "Finding One's Own Voice," 33.

CHAPTER TWO

Roots and Bridges:

The Kitchen and the Trilogy (*Chicken Soup with Barley, Roots, I'm Talking about Jerusalem*)

The five plays that established Arnold Wesker as a significant new force in the British theater were all written before he agreed to become artistic director of Centre 42 in 1961, and with hindsight they can be seen to have led logically toward that decisive moment in his career. Looking back on the impact made by the first performances of the Trilogy, *The Kitchen,* and *Chips with Everything* between 1958 and 1962, it is also possible to understand the nature of their appeal to contemporary audiences and reviewers.[1] Although John Osborne's *Look Back in Anger* had been greeted by Kenneth Tynan as "the best young play of its decade"—a play that was said to present "post-war youth as it really is"—it was not long before Wesker's Trilogy was being lauded with equal enthusiasm by A. R. Jones as "a profoundly moving embodiment in imaginative terms of his generation's experience of the history of our time."[2] This early sense of the importance of Wesker's achievement on sociological as well as artistic grounds has been endorsed by John Orr in a more recent estimate of its place in the cultural evolution of modern Britain: "Wesker's trilogy is the most powerful composite dramatic statement in the post-war English theatre. It gives a multitudinous voice to the lower-class English, urban and rural, and with a magnificent ear for the demotic."[3]

In spite of the initial tendency to associate Wesker with other young dramatists who emerged in the late 1950s, his distinctive contribution was soon recognized by Henry Goodman, "A political dramatist in the tradition of the thirties, Wesker uses the stage as a platform and a pulpit for the New Left; in this respect he is more outspoken and probably farther left than his compatriots."[4] But for all his political earnestness, Wesker's "great capacity for revealing tenderness and hurt" also engaged the attention of John Kershaw, and the Trilogy has been highly valued by Katharine Worth as "a bleak and tender recording of the ordinary pains of life."[5]

Wesker's technical approach in his first two plays offered as much of a challenge to contemporary expectations as did the social focus of his material and the political orientation of his message. *The Kitchen,* with a cast of thirty named characters, "broke most of the rules of dramatic construction by assuming that human activity could be reproduced on the stage in full, with little basic plot"; and *Chicken Soup with Barley,* though conventional in having "a single line of action and a series of built-up climaxes and curtain-lines," exploits the methods of cinema in its rapid movement across the years from 1936 to 1956, while "off-stage, outside the set, a complex activity of filmic proportions is always in process."[6] The playwright himself acknowledged in an interview in 1959 that the audacity of his dramaturgy, which many found so stimulating, was a consequence of his lack of experience: "It was one advantage of being theatrically uneducated. I was not frightened of anything."[7]

For the reader and spectator in the 1990s, these apprentice works raise central questions both about Wesker's own intentions and achievements as a dramatist and about the nature of an art that is committed to the service of an ideal of social change. Such an art must offer the words and actions of its characters as representative of social groups and political stances, but if it does not at the same time imbue them with sufficient passion and individuality, they can too easily be dismissed as the lifeless exemplars of a theoretical view of the world. From the beginning, Wesker sought ways of deriving his political message from the experiences of the people whose lives he presented on the stage, rather than devising characters to embody preconceived ideas. *The Kitchen* has been described as "at once realistic and representative" in its dramatization of the human activity behind the scenes in a large restaurant, a daring technique that contrives to contain the "documentary realism" of its re-creation of the large-scale preparation and serving of food within a form "that verges upon the expressionistic."[8]

The problem of accommodating content to effective form, and both to an ideological purpose, is complicated in Wesker's case by the fact that each of his first five plays drew heavily and directly on autobiographical sources—*The Kitchen* and *Chips with Everything* on his experiences of the worlds of work and the armed services, and the Trilogy on details of the personal histories and circumstances of himself and his wife and members of their respective families. The unease, even embarrassment, that has been expressed about certain incidents in these early plays suggests that the author's closeness to the raw material of his art resulted in an occasional failure to transform the personally significant into the dramatically convincing. To explain, as Wesker does in response to one of the criticisms leveled at his work by Ronald Hayman, that the game with the umbrella in *I'm Talking about Jerusalem* ''actually happened—it isn't something that I invented''[9] may do little to alter the verdict that biographical detail has not been adequately digested into art, but it does point to one of the strengths of a dramatist who insists on this kind of straightforward truth to experience. This strength, which results in the ''setting of political thought at the level of the texture of life,''[10] saves him from falling too often, even in these early plays, into two of the dangers identified by Hayman: that of ''the separation that sometimes occurs between action and argument'' and that of ''using his characters and their situation to make points that were preoccupying him long before they were.''[11]

The Kitchen (1959, revised 1961)

In the introduction to the printed text of his first play, Wesker himself asserts the inseparability of the specific and the universal in his perception of one particular ''slice of life'': ''The world might have been a stage for Shakespeare but to me it is a kitchen, where people come and go and cannot stay long enough to understand each other, and friendships, loves and enmities are forgotten as quickly as they are made'' (5; 2:9). Leeming and Trussler go further and recognize that it is this primary fidelity to the ''texture'' of the daily round in a kitchen that allows its wider political significance to be released and renders it ''simultaneously a dramatic metaphor for industrial capitalist society, and a very specific and closely specified place.''[12] The setting is, in fact, more important than either individual characterization or plot; the play takes its shape from and gives expression to the workers' corporate experience of a single working day, in which they are driven to peaks of frenetic activity by the demand for midday and evening meals. As both "dramatic metaphor" and "closely specified place," the kitchen itself embodies two of the central themes that run through this early group of plays and reappear from time to time in later works.

The first is the insight, associated especially with naturalism as a theatrical mode, that human responses are shaped and distorted by the pressure of the social environment. As the kitchen staff assembles at the start of a new day, Wesker quickly establishes the tensions created by the artificial conditions under which men and women from diverse cultural and linguistic backgrounds are forced into close proximity, with no purpose to give them a sense of common identity beyond the imperative to earn a weekly wage. Professional bickering between a Jewish vegetable cook and a Cypriot in charge of the cold buffet soon flares into racial antagonism, and much of the desultory conversation among the staff revolves around a violent quarrel the previous evening between Peter and Gaston, "a bloody German" and "a lousy Cypro." One of the pastry cooks shrugs off the latter incident philosophically: "There's always fights, who knows how they begin?" (18; 2:19). Dimitri, a kitchen porter and therefore very low in the hierarchy of this social microcosm, offers a more psychologically perceptive and politically meaningful explanation: "Listen, you put a man in the plate-room all day he's got dishes to make clean, and stinking bins to take away, and floors to sweep, what else there is for him to do—he want to fight. He got to show he is a man some way. So—blame him!'' (19; 2:20). Peter himself acknowledges that human beings are capable of adapting to the economic necessity represented by the intractable reality of the kitchen—"We all said we wouldn't last the day, but tell me what is there a man can't get used to? Nothing! You forget where you are and you say it's a job'' (36; 2:34)—but he is also aware of the metaphorical status of this alienating environment: "This—this madhouse it's always here. When you go, when I go, when Dimitri go—this kitchen stays. It'll go on when we die, think about that. . . . You and the kitchen. And the kitchen don't mean nothing to you and you don't mean to the kitchen nothing'' (53; 2:48). In the theater, there is no escape for the audience any more than for the characters from the alien and alienating existence of the kitchen, which dominates the activity and affects the behavior of those whose only function is to serve it and to sustain with their labor the economic system it represents. Before a word is spoken, the night porter *"lights the ovens,"* which emit a *"hum"* as the flame *"settles into a steady burn."* Wesker's stage directions are explicit: *"It is a noise that will stay with us to the end. As he lights each oven, the noise grows from a small to a loud ferocious roar. There will be this continuous battle between the dialogue and the noise of the ovens. The Producer must work out his own balance"* (13; 2:15). Much of the theatrical impact of the play's climax derives from the moment of complete silence following the *"slow hiss"* as *"all the fires of the ovens die down,"* when Peter cuts through the gas pipe in an act of instinctive rebellion against the relentless and dehumanizing demands of the environment in which he is condemned to pass the majority of his waking hours.

The second theme of the play is the human need for something more satisfying than the monotonous routine of wage labor. Before the accelerating rhythm of the kitchen's day sweeps everyone up into the frenzy of the lunchtime rush, there is time for sexual banter, for brief exchanges about such off-duty enthusiasms as motorbike engines and homemade radios, and for nostalgic reminiscences about the wonders of New York. It is in the interlude between parts 1 and 2, however, during an afternoon break in which the sounds of the oven are reduced to half, that the stifled impulses to create and to communicate struggle for expression.[13] Peter, who has just been accused of being a dreamer by Hans, constructs a precarious triumphal archway from dustbins, saucepans, and a broom and decorates it with dishcloths. Kevin, an Irish newcomer to the kitchen, mocks him for playing like a child, and Peter challenges them all to liberate themselves from the drabness of the present by telling their dreams: ''This one says games and that one says dreams. You think it's a waste of time? You know what a game is? A dream? It's the time when you forget what you are and you make what you could be. When a man dreams—he grows, big, better'' (55; 2:49). This passage provides an important gloss on the many games and rituals that Wesker's characters engage in throughout his work.[14] It is often by playing games, particularly games that depend on cooperation among the participants, that individuals are able to transcend the selfishness and the loneliness that a competitive society encourages and imposes upon them, and to experience, if only for the duration of the game, the sense of community that derives from the pursuit of a common goal. Peter's words are also an early statement of Wesker's belief in the power of the imagination to inspire human beings in the practical task of building a better future. Toward the end of *I'm Talking about Jerusalem*, Ronnie Kahn accuses his brother-in-law of betraying his earlier vision of fulfillment through pride in craftsmanship. Dave Simmonds, beaten by the economics of mass production and the shoddy values of consumerism, turns on him angrily with the same charge that Kevin leveled at Peter, "You child you—visions don't work." But Ronnie desperately, and with a passion that overrides mere logic, insists on the need for visions, even in the face of defeat and disillusionment: "They *do* work! And even if they don't work then for God's sake let's try and behave as though they do—or else nothing will work" (222; 1:216). Predictably, the imaginations of Peter's fellow workers, stunted by lack of education and the boredom of repetitive tasks, find it hard to pursue dreams beyond "Money! Money! Money!" and "Women!" and a shed in which to tinker with radios and television sets. The pastry cook, Paul, however, speaks of a deeper need for human contact that is frustrated by the impersonal routines and shallow antagonisms of the work place. Admitting that he doesn't like Peter, he gropes toward the possibility of greater understanding:

> All right! But now it's quiet, the ovens are low, the work has stopped for a little and now I'm getting to know you. I still think you're a pig—only now, not so much of a pig. So that's what I dream. I dream of a friend. You give me a rest, you give me silence, you take away this mad kitchen so I make friends, so I think—maybe all the people I thought were pigs are not so much pigs. (57; 2:51)

To illustrate his new insight, he relates an incident that exposed the frightening intolerance of his next-door neighbor—

"he's my age, married and got two kids"—a bus driver with whom he has been on nodding terms for years. The irrational hatred engendered in the neighbor, an ordinary man, by a recent peace march brings Paul face to face with the human consequences of a divisive social system and leads him to the brink of political consciousness in the recognition that things must be changed: "And the horror is this—that there's a wall, a big wall between me and millions of people like him. And I think—where will it end? What do you do about it?" (58; 2:52).

Laurence Kitchin has written admiringly of the interlude, which slowly and naturally builds toward the climax of Paul's speech: "This wonderful scene, with the ovens at half-power, a guitar playing, and men of limited intellect fumbling with the issues which convulse the mid-century world, is a masterpiece by any standard."[15] Certainly, the texture of Wesker's writing here can be used to refute the criticism that his characters are devised as mouthpieces for predigested arguments. The painful process by which Paul arrives *not* at an answer but at the question that is the prerequisite for political thought—"What do you do about it?"—carries complete dramatic conviction. Equally convincing is Peter's refusal to reveal his own dream and the violent destruction of the carefully constructed archway of pots and pans in part 2 that accompanies his confession: "I can't dream in a kitchen!" (70; 2:61). The later eruption of frustrated and futile aggression, which serves only to bewilder the restaurant owner, Marango, who is as much a blind instrument of the system as Peter himself, has the full weight of the play's painstaking exposition of the German cook's social and psychological predicament behind it.[16] Action and argument are united in an event that grows naturalistically from the conjunction of specific character and situation and that at the same time reverberates with a more general and political significance.

Chicken Soup with Barley (1958) and *I'm Talking about Jerusalem* (1960)

The Trilogy, of which *Roots* has proved to be the most successful constituent,[17] embodies Wesker's attempt to explore the human and political complexities of the problems implicit in the two questions thrown up by the conversation and the dramatic action of his first play: Paul's "What do you do about it?" and Marango's forlornly repeated response to Peter's concluding act of sabotage, "What is there more?" The members of the Kahn family, who take center stage in *Chicken Soup with Barley* and *I'm Talking about Jerusalem,* are more ideologically aware, more politically involved, and above all more articulate than the polyglot cast of cooks, dishwashers, and waitresses in *The Kitchen.* As East End Jews who are active in the Communist party and the trades unions, their private and public lives are by no means typical of the British working classes. Michael Anderson's description opens up both their collective character and their special function in Wesker's dramatic study of the dilemmas of the left in postwar Britain, "The Kahns are unusual people; the same passionate emotionalism with which their family life is charged permeates the various brands of socialism which dominate their actions." In marked contrast, Beatie's family of agricultural laborers in the middle play of the Trilogy "are representative of the non-political majority: in the Bryant household there is no passion and no ideology."[18] It is this difference that makes *Roots* "the lynch-pin of the trilogy,"[19] since the goal of the social and economic revolution to which Sarah Kahn commits her energies and idealism is, for her son Ronnie and for the playwright himself, primarily a means to the enrichment of the lives of the culturally undernourished and underprivileged.[20] One of the things that makes the Trilogy such an impressive achievement is the courage and the insight with which Wesker takes into full dramatic account the experiences and attitudes of the inarticulate, stolid, and uncomprehending Bryants as well as the talkative, volatile, and intellectually alert Kahns.

As a sequence, the three plays do not form a conventional trilogy, in which a story is pursued chronologically. *Roots* and *I'm Talking about Jerusalem* branch off at different historical junctures from the narrative trunk of the Kahn family saga initially presented in *Chicken Soup with Barley*. Each of the three plays contains allusions to the parts of the action dramatized in more detail in the others, but the disposition of material is governed more by the progress of a developing debate about the nature and experience of socialism than by the demands of narrative completeness or coherence.[21] *Chicken Soup with Barley* is clearly structured by the historic milestones of the local and international contest with Fascism in 1936 (in London against Oswald Mosley's British blackshirts and in Spain against Franco) and the traumatic effect on Western Communists of the suppression of the popular rising in Hungary by Russian tanks in 1956. Halfway between these events, which dominate acts 1 and 3, the two scenes of the middle act specify the immediately postwar years of 1946 and 1947. During that middle act, Harry slides into unemployment, lethargy, and sickness; the adolescent Ronnie becomes excited over the early measures of the new Labour government and develops an ambition to write "socialist novels"; and Dave and Ada become disillusioned with "the splendid and heroic working class" (41; 1:42) and decide to cultivate their own version of socialism in the countryside, where they plan to escape the consequences of industrial capitalism by producing handmade furniture, in effect reviving ancient traditions of craftsmanship and self-sufficiency. Near the beginning of act 3, in November 1955, it is made clear that Harry has been paralysed by a second stroke, Ada and Dave "are still in the country," and Ronnie is working as a cook in Paris. *Roots* is located not long before this final act, when Ronnie is still in London and Harry is already an invalid. *I'm Talking about Jerusalem* opens with the arrival in Norfolk of Ada and Dave Simmonds in 1946 and ends with their packing to return to London in 1959 on a day that symbolically links the collapse of their personal experiment with the failure of socialist politics at a national level as they hear news on the radio of the Conservative party's election for a third successive term of government.

Wesker has explained that the twenty-three-year time span of the entire Trilogy was a result of his "obsession with digging back as far as possible to beginnings, in order to explain the present."[22] For Wesker's generation, those beginnings were to be traced to the 1930s, and the evocation of one memorable day in that decade occupies the first act of *Chicken Soup with Barley* and lays the foundations for much that will follow. The Kahns' basement in the East End of London is alive with purposeful activity. The house and the streets outside echo with the sounds of people who have a sure sense of communal identity and of the contribution that they are making to the steady march of history. In scene 1, feelings run high at the prospect of opposing a rally by Mosley's Fascists, and both nationally and internationally the ideological lines are clearly drawn for committed Communists like Dave Simmonds: "Spain is the battle-front. Spain is a real issue at last" (14; 1:16). Monty Blatt, another young activist, can scarcely contain his exhilaration: "Bloody wonderful, isn't it? Makes you feel proud, eh Sarah? Every section of this working-class area that we've approached has responded. The dockers at Limehouse have come out to the man." (17; 1:19). Later in the day, they all return in triumph from the barricades, bubbling over with confidence in the future:

> PRINCE: There's no turning back now—nothing can stop the workers now.
> MONTY: I bet we have a revolution soon. Hitler won't stop at Spain, you know. . . . Then *we'll* move in. (25; 1:26–27)

Even in the midst of this carnival of hope and solidarity, there are ominous signs of tension among the comrades and within the family. The hotheaded Monty and the more disciplined Prince disagree about tactics, and later Sarah clashes with her sister-in-law over the behavior of Harry and with the young men over the principles upon which political activity should be based: "Love comes now. You have to start with love. How can you talk about socialism otherwise?" (28; 1:30). But this belief proves ineffectual in Sarah's relations with her own husband, who justifiably accuses her of nagging. The fact that her complaints about Harry are themselves justified—he steals money from her purse and takes refuge at his mother's during the anti-Fascist demonstration—only serves to complicate the domestic situation. An act that began with subdued bickering between husband and wife closes on a violent note with Sarah hurling accusations and crockery after a retreating Harry and then turning to comfort her daughter, while little Ronnie *"stands watching them—listening and bewildered"* (34; 1:35).

True to the naturalistic doctrine of the twin influences of nature and culture, heredity and environment, the personalities of the elder Kahns loom over the development of their children and changing social and economic conditions in Britain, together with political events in Eastern Europe, undermine the clear-cut idealism of act 1. The adolescent Ronnie of act 2 voices his secret dread after a row with his devious and weak-willed father, "I watch you and I see myself and I'm terrified" (56; 1:56). The rest of the Trilogy confirms these fears with the loss of his socialist faith and the abandonment of the woman he loves. By the final act of *I'm Talking about Jerusalem,* he has slipped into the self-pitying attitude of his despised father: "I can't keep a job and I can't keep a girl so everyone thinks what I say doesn't count. Like they used to say of Dad. Poor old Harry—poor old Ronnie" (214; 1:208). Ada, by contrast, has Sarah's resilience and iron will. She may not share the simple Communist creed that sustains her mother through every domestic and political disaster, but once she and Dave have committed themselves to their own vision of a better life, she takes each setback with the courage and firmness that are her most valuable inheritance from Sarah: "You say I'm like her? You're right. I'm also strong, I shall survive every battle that faces me too, and this place means survival for me. We—are—staying—put!'' (200; 1:195).

The conditions under which the comrades of act 1 of *Chicken Soup with Barley* find themselves living as the years pass take their inevitable toll. Dave's illusions have been shattered by his experiences during the Second World War, when he fought alongside men who ''did not know what the war was about'' and who enjoyed the chance ''to get away from their wives in order to behave like animals'' (41; 1:42); and Ada's long wait for him to return has reinforced her political impatience with the empty ''claptrap'' of party slogans and has alienated her from her youthful mission to change the world. In a series of vivid clashes with Harry, Ronnie, and Sarah in the second act of *Chicken Soup with Barley,* it is Ada Kahn who opens up the debate about the moral authority and practical effectiveness of socialism that lies at the heart of the Trilogy. Wesker gives Ada an opportunity to explain her new vision of the family as an economic unit, in which work and life are ''part of one existence,'' and to deflate her brother's callow enthusiasm for ''town and country planning'': ''I do not believe in the right to organize people. And anyway I'm not so sure that I love them enough to *want* to organize them'' (40–41; 1:41). But this does not mean that the dramatist endorses the views of his character. Sarah joins in the argument to brand Ada's ideal of self-fulfillment as a coward's solution and takes issue with the terms in which she has rationalized her indifference or hostility to other people: ''So what, we shouldn't care any more? We must all run away?'' In reply, Ada reminds her mother of the contradiction between her principle of universal love and the misery of her own flawed relationship with her husband: "Care! Care! What right have we to care? How can we care for a world outside ourselves when the world inside is in disorder? . . . What audacity tells you you can harbour a billion people in a theory?" (42–43; 1:43). Scenes of this kind demonstrate the force of Wesker's claim that the spectacle of "people caught up in an actual argument about ideas can be essentially dramatic,"[23] especially when full measure is granted to the personalities of the participants and the richly created context in which the discussion takes place. By rooting Ada's theoretical stance firmly in the realities of her domestic history— "All her life Mummy's had to put up with this. I shall be glad to get away" (40; 1:41), she tells the work-shy Harry— the playwright has engineered a complex dramatic experience for the audience in which intellectual preferences and human sympathy may be at odds with each other.

The two scenes of act 3 explore two different kinds of defection from the ideals of act 1, compromise and despair, which contrast with Dave and Ada's more positive attempt to build an alternative to the values of the postwar world. In the first, Monty Blatt and his wife visit Sarah and Harry in the London County Council flat that has been their home since the war. Monty's "little shop up north" now provides him with "a comfortable living," and he is no longer a member of the party. Disillusioned like so many prewar activists by events in Spain and Stalin's Russia and shamed by Sarah's dogged refusal to let go of her faith, he defends his retreat into middle-class respectability and quietism:

> MONTY: There's nothing more to life than a house, some friends, and a family—take my word.

SARAH: And when someone drops an atom bomb on
your family?
MONTY [*pleading*]: So what can I do—tell me?
There's nothing I can do any more. I'm too small;
who can I trust? It's a big, lousy world of mad politicians—I can't trust them, Sarah. (62; 1:62)

In a speech that leaves the audience once again caught between contradictory responses, Monty puts his finger on the
intellectual shortcomings and the human strength of Sarah's
lifelong commitment to a political ideal: "For her the world
is black and white. . . . Do you think she ever read a book
on political economy in her life? Bless her! Someone told her
socialism was happiness so she joined the Party" (62–63;
1:62). Wesker's dramatic dialectic continues, as Sarah
quickly deflates Monty's nostalgia for the communal spirit
and the shining certainties of act 1—"Everyone in the East
End was going somewhere. . . . The East End was a big
mother"—with a sharp reminder of the other side of the Depression: "Horrible times—dirty, unclean, cheating!" (63;
1:62–63). But in the next scene, the sounds of a domestic
quarrel in the courtyard below call attention to the positive
values of that "big mother," which have been swept away
with the dirt of the prewar slums. Harry's sister, now retired
from her job as a trade-union organizer, comments on the human cost of replacing the old social environment: "There's
always something happening in these flats. Last week a
woman tried to gas herself. . . . These flats are a world on
their own. You live a whole lifetime here and not know your
next-door neighbour" (68; 1:67–68).

The latter part of this scene brings the play to its emotional
and intellectual climax with Ronnie's return from Paris to

confront his mother with the failure of the creed she has taught him to live by: "You didn't tell me there were any doubts. . . . Were we cheated or did we cheat ourselves?" (72–73; 1:71–72). Sarah resents his accusation that she is unmoved by the news from Hungary and by reports of anti-Semitic crimes in the Soviet Union, but she clings to her conviction, which is more emotional than rational, that the greatest battle is against indifference and nihilism. For her, "the idea of brotherhood" is based not on the abstractions of "philosophy" but on concrete examples of human love in action, like a neighbor's present of chicken soup with barley, which once saved Ada's life when Harry was thoughtlessly squandering the family's relief money on salt-beef sandwiches for himself. The play ends with a counterpoint between Sarah's insistent plea, "You've got to care, you've got to care or you'll die," and Ronnie's echo of Monty's defeatism before the size of the problems facing humanity—"it's too big, not yet—it's too big to care for it" (77; 1:75).

Whereas the first part of the Trilogy charts the painful retreat of an entire social group from the hopes and political certainties of 1936, the third part follows the doomed progress of the attempt to forge an alternative way of life by one idealistic couple. But although it ends in apparent defeat, the dramatic impetus of *I'm Talking about Jerusalem* is more positive than that of *Chicken Soup with Barley*. In the earlier play, the schoolboy Ronnie had boasted of a quality that marked him as a member of the Kahn clan: "Mother, my one virtue—if I got any at all—is that I always imagine you can solve things by talking about them" (45; 1:45). The Simmondses no longer believe that the world can be changed by discussions and public rhetoric. Dave refuses to explain their decision to leave the city and abandon politics, "Nothing's wrong with socialism Sarah, only we want to live it—not talk about it"; and Ada adds, "At last something more than just words" (166–67; 1:164–65). Ten years later, a conversation with aunts Esther and Cissie provokes Dave into a fierce defense of his already failing project to maintain the dignity of labor: "I talked enough! You bloody Kahns you! You all talk. Sarah, Ronnie, all of you. I talked enough! I wanted to do something. Hands I've got—you see them? I wanted to do something" (211; 1:205). But even though Dave eventually admits that the contradictions between individualism and socialism are irreconcilable—"Maybe Sarah's right, maybe you can't build on your own" (222; 1:216)—he and Ada remain morally and spiritually unbroken. Unlike the embittered Libby Dobson, a wartime friend of Dave's who visits them in act 2,[24] and unlike the self-pitying Ronnie of act 3, who cannot cope with a world that does not match up to his high expectations, Dave and Ada are busy preparing for a new start in London at the close of the play: "It's not all that bad. We came here, we worked hard, we've loved every minute of it and we're still young" (221; 1:216).

This resilience of the central characters is reflected in a dramatic orchestration that also reflects their denunciation of talking as a substitute for living. In striking contrast to *Chicken Soup with Barley,* which characteristically brings the curtain down on a negative image of disorder or humiliation—quarrels between husband and wife or father and son, Harry's first stroke and his attack of incontinence, Ronnie's despair—almost every scene in *I'm Talking about Jerusalem* ends with a ritual of reconciliation, which answers conflict

40

and disappointment not with verbal argument but with physical gestures of human solidarity and understanding. The closing moments of the first scene bring the fractured family together in the shared simplicities of unpacking and washing up and the cultural bonding of a Yiddish folk song; the double trauma of Dobson's subversive mockery and Dave's dismissal from his temporary job at the farm is soothed by a dressing-up game, in which Dave drapes his wife in a large red towel, offers her an olive branch, and kneels in homage to her—a charade that allows the curtain to fall on gently shared laughter rather than recriminations and tears; the desertion of Dave's apprentice for better-paid work in a factory and Ada's return from a harrowing visit to her dying father are countered by the game with their little boy, which brings the scene to a magical and affirmative conclusion: "Now you are a real human being Daniel who can look and think and talk and you can come out and slay the lions" (202; 1:197).

Roots (1959)

Standing at the heart of the Trilogy, flanked by studies of disintegration and failure, *Roots* proclaims the possibility of entering into the full human inheritance toward which Dave and Ada are leading their son. Over the three years of their love affair, Ronnie has been trying to teach Beatie Bryant the lesson embodied in the game played by the Simmonds family. As Beatie reports to her mother, " 'Talk,' he say, 'and look and listen and think and ask questions' " (115; 1:115). It is above all learning to talk that will emancipate Beatie into a richer experience of life. Wesker is preoccupied with the

41

familiar midcentury theme of language and communication in this central play of the Trilogy, but his position is quite different from that of many of his contemporaries. Martin Esslin has charted the ways in which some of the dramatists of the 1950s strove to express their "sense of the senselessness of the human condition and the inadequacy of the rational approach by the open abandonment of rational devices and discursive thought." As a consequence, writers like Samuel Beckett, Eugene Ionesco, and Harold Pinter developed a Theater of the Absurd, which "tends toward a radical devaluation of language, toward a poetry that is to emerge from the concrete and objectified images of the stage itself."[25] Early in his career, the author of *Waiting for Godot* had explained that for him "art is the apotheosis of solitude," since human beings are trapped in the subjective universe inside their own heads. If "the only world that has reality and significance" is "the world of our own latent consciousness," then words are ineffectual as a means of sharing ideas and experiences, "There is no communication because there are no vehicles of communication."[26] For Ionesco, the language of society prevents meaningful contact between one mind and another because it "is nothing but clichés, empty formulas and slogans."[27] Neither Wesker's rationalism nor his socialism permitted him to endorse the solipsistic and nihilistic tendencies of the absurdist movement, but Ada Kahn comes close to some of its attitudes. Her skepticism about the efficacy of language erupts in her attack on "the meaningless titles" bestowed on enemies of the party in the "threepenny pamphlet"—"bourgeois intellectual," "Trotskyist," "reactionary Social Democrat" (41; 1:42)—and in her refusal to discuss her retreat from politics with Sarah: "Because language isn't any use! Because we talk about one thing and you hear another that's why'' (166; 1:164). She later confronts the emotional as distinct from the political consequences of a breakdown in communication as she thinks back over her relationship with her dying father:

perhaps I didn't tell him I loved him. Useless bloody things words are. Ronnie and his bridges! ''Words are bridges,'' he wrote, ''to get from one place to another.'' Wait till he's older and he learns about silences—they span worlds. (199; 1:194)

Ronnie's image of words as bridges, however, is the key to a positive view of language, which offers a solution to the problem that Paul became aware of in *The Kitchen* and expressed in the negative image of ''a big wall'' dividing one human being from another. The centrality of the bridge symbolism in *Roots* is established by its prominence in Beatie's first account of Ronnie's sermons about life and values:

''Well, language is words,'' he'd say, as though he were telling me a secret. ''It's bridges, so that you can get safely from one place to another. And the more bridges you know about the more places you can see!'' . . . So then he'd say: ''Bridges! bridges! bridges! Use your bridges woman. It took thousands of years to build them, use them!'' (88; 1:90)

Wesker's evocation of the social and linguistic environment in which Beatie grew up has long been recognized as one of the artistic triumphs of *Roots*.[28] The world of the Bryants is one in which words are an undemanding accompaniment to the routines of work and domestic life. Conversation in the cottage of the Beales, the sister and brother-in-law with whom Beatie stays in act 1, revolves around Jimmy's recurrent indigestion, tidbits of information about members of the local community, the vegetables in Jimmy's allotment, family squabbles, and childhood reminiscences. Well-tried verbal formulas serve their turn and no topic is pursued for more than a few moments. A stage direction describes the relation between speech and the wide range of physical activities that occupy the characters: *"BEATIE helps collect dishes from table and proceeds to help wash up. This is a silence that needs organizing. Throughout the play there is no sign of intense living from any of the characters—BEATIE's bursts are the exception. . . . They talk in fits and starts mainly as a sort of gossip"* (90; 1:92).[29] When Beatie disturbs their complacency with her unconventional life-style or with a direct challenge to their unexamined assumptions—like "love in the afternoon" or the futility of "playing soldiers" at weekends in the age of the hydrogen bomb—they hurriedly change the subject or stop the argument dead in its tracks, "Don't you come pushin' ideas across at us—we're all right as we are" (92; 1:94). Later in the play, when Beatie has moved to the parental home, Mr. Bryant will bear ample witness to his wife's judgment that "he don't ever talk more'n he hev to" (121; 1:121); and Mrs. Bryant herself will lose patience with her daughter's attempt to engage her in sustained discussion about the difference between a folk song and pop music:

> BEATIE: Mother, I'm *talking* to you. Blust woman it's not often we get together and really talk, it's nearly always me listening to you telling who's dead. Just listen a second.

MRS BRYANT: Well go on gal, but you always take so long to say it. (114; 1:114)

Beatie's repeated efforts to stir her relatives from the mental lethargy that makes them such easy prey to economic and cultural exploitation are met with hostility, incomprehension, and ridicule. At one point, her mother is provoked into defending the limited horizons that Wesker had exposed in *The Kitchen:* "I fed you. I clothed you. I took you out to the sea. What more d'you want. We're only country folk you know" (128; 1:127). The answer is supplied from the repertoire of Ronnie's sayings that Beatie carries round in her head: " 'Christ,' he say. 'Socialism isn't talking all the time, it's living, it's singing, it's dancing, it's being interested in what go on around you, it's being concerned about people and the world' " (129; 1:129).

However critical Beatie may be of her family, the dramatist himself is far from condemning or blaming the section of the rural community that they represent. He has more than once been accused of adopting a patronizing attitude and of displaying what John McGrath has branded as "a lamentable ignorance of the strengths and values of the working class itself."[30] Wesker has insisted that he writes from first-hand knowledge and from direct personal involvement in the issues raised in these early plays: "*I've* always spoken about what the working man *could* be and felt anger that he's abused for what he *is;* and in doing this it was necessary to tell him what he is as I know him from experience. He's *my* class and my background and therefore what I say I say from love and a concern for wasted lives."[31] Nevertheless, for all the genuine care and the naturalistic brilliance with which he has created a stage image of the stolid existence of the Beales and the Bryants, the play's center of gravity lies elsewhere.

It has become a commonplace of criticism to praise the theatrical impact of the heroine's transformation in the closing sequence of act 3, as if Ronnie's letter had miraculously shocked her into articulateness. Beatie may experience the flood of energy with which her strong spirit rallies from the two-fold blow of her lover's betrayal and her mother's vindictive gloating as a liberation and an awakening—"I'm talking. Jenny, Frankie, Mother—I'm not quoting no more. . . . God in heaven, *Ronnie!* It does work, it's happening to me, I can feel it's happened, I'm beginning, on my own two feet—I'm beginning. . . . " (150; 1:148); but she has always had a higher charge of natural vitality than the rest of her family, and she has been moving slowly and surely toward this moment of conscious emancipation since the play began. Her sister, Jenny, comments on the energy with which she bustles about, tidying up the cottage, "You hit this place like a bloody whirlwind you do" (99; 1:100). Even Mrs. Bryant, whose drab daily routine is measured by the passing of buses and tradesmen's vans, responds to her daughter's invigorating presence—"Thank God you come home sometimes gal—you do bring a little life with you anyway" (116; 1:116)—and is caught up in the enthusiasm of her joyous dance to the music of Bizet, which brings act 2 to its climax. She may inherit some of her mother's stubbornness, but as Tom Costello has pointed out, the process dramatized in Beatie's growth toward independence has both social and psychological implications that undermine the philosophical foundations of "classical naturalism": "Man is not necessarily a determined victim of environment or heredity, nor is he a passive sufferer who cannot change the world."[32]

It would be unjust to the honesty of Wesker's vision and the subtlety of his dramaturgy, however, to conclude, as one critic does, that the Bryant family "is wrong," while "Beatie, because she stands against it, is clearly right"; and that the views of Ronnie Kahn, "who has made her what she is, even though he lets her down so badly at the end," are to be endorsed without question.[33] Other commentators have been more open to the complex nature of what *Roots* has to offer as a dramatic experience. Costello, for example, argues that the function of Beatie's practice of quoting her lover's words is "to create an other-than-present-tense consciousness," and by this means the values and opinions that Wesker shares with his absent character "are kept at an aesthetic distance from the realities and limitations of the naturalistic immediate moment and so retain their purity as a distinct idealism."[34] The theatricality of Beatie's performance—she more than once stands on a chair to declaim her memorized lines—also forces the theater audience to include the reactions of her on-stage audience in its own reception of Ronnie's ideas. The occasional laughter raised at his expense by the dry wit or incomprehension of the Bryant clan allows the positive content of his speeches to be registered while the pretentiousness of his stance is suitably deflated. The Beales remark early on, "He don' believe in hevin' much fun then?" and "He sound a queer bor to me" (87; 1:88–89); and Mrs. Bryant cannot conceal her dismay at the pompous style of the dicta that Beatie repeats: "He *talk* like that? . . . Sounds like a preacher" (110; 1:111); "Blust he talk like a book'' (129; 1:128). Ronnie's solution to the moral problem posed by the parable of the girl and the ferryman is greeted by a chorus of derisive comments: ''He've got it all worked out then!''; ''He's sure of himself then?''; ''He think everyone is gonna listen then?''; ''Hark at that then'' (143; 1:141). Even Beatie, when she finds her own voice at the end, cuts through the sentimentality that colors the urban intellectual's idealization of those who work on the land: ''Oh, *he* thinks we count all right—living in mystic communion with nature. Living in mystic bloody communion with nature (indeed)'' (149; 1:147).

Furthermore, as Jacqueline Latham has demonstrated, the dramatist does not only qualify the negative view of Beatie's family by using this kind of subversive irony to ''achieve an alienation effect'' and ''subject his ideas to self-criticism''; he is also at pains to present positive aspects of the rural way of life in more concrete terms. While Ronnie's romanticism may be misplaced, there is no doubt that the agricultural worker's daily contact with the primary processes of nature breeds a healthy matter-of-factness and ''a compassion which has not been blunted by this familiarity.''[35] Jimmy Beales relates with unruffled good humor how he coped when Stan Mann ''messed his pants'' in the allotment, ''I put the ole hose over him and brought him home along the fields with an ole sack around his waist'' (101; 1:102). Beatie responds by confessing that she ''can't touch'' Ronnie's paralysed father, who also suffers from senile incontinence: ''I can't bear sick men. They smell'' (102; 1:103). The Bryants take the news of their old neighbor's subsequent death with an impassiveness that belies neither their affection for the individual nor their acceptance of the inevitability of nature's cycle: ''He were a

good ole bor though. Yes he was. A good ole stick. There!''
(119; 1:119). Beatie's more squeamish reaction—''Oh hell, I
hate dying''—again indicates the extent to which she has already lost touch with her community's sense of harmony with
the natural order in which disease and death are as unavoid-
able as the imminent farrowing of "the ole sow" (118;
1:118). In the same way, Ronnie's encouragement of Beatie's
new mode of self-expression in her abstract painting is to be
set alongside reminders that the creative instinct has not been
completely extinguished in the other Bryant women, in spite
of their lonely hours of drudgery in homes that lack the con-
veniences of modern life. Mrs. Bryant brightens her front
room with flowers in pots and vases, and there is a flash of
pride in the questions with which she welcomes her daughter:
''Did you see my flowers as you come in? Got some of my
hollyhocks still flowering. Creeping up the wall they are—
did you catch a glimpse on 'em? And my asters and gerani-
ums? (109; 1:110); and Jenny produces *"a most beautiful-
looking plaited loaf of bread"* from the oven with a similar
glow of self-satisfaction, ''Isn't that beautiful Beatie?'' (96;
1:97).

It is typical of Wesker's insight, and vital to the complexity
of the final scene, that the unexpected arrival of Ronnie's letter should trigger an unusual degree of articulateness in the
mother, as well as in the daughter who has spent much of the
past fortnight finding fault with the world in which she grew
up. The shock of the slap that she administers to Beatie's
face releases Mrs. Bryant's pent up feelings of hurt and resentment and frustration:

I hed enough. All this time she've bin home she've bin
tellin' me I didn't do this and I didn't do that and I hevn't

49

understood half what she've said and I've hed enough. . . . She think I like it, she do! Thinks I like it being cooped up in this house all day. Well I'm telling you my gal—I don't! There! And if I had a chance to be away working somewhere the whole lot on you's could go to hell—the lot on you's. (146–47; 1:144–45)

It is in direct response to her mother's challenge—"you say you know something we don't so *you* do the talking"—that Beatie is goaded into explaining what she means by "roots." The meaning she discovers in the process of talking goes far beyond naturalism's conception of the determining influences of environment and heredity and Ronnie's romantic notion of life close to the soil. What Wesker dramatizes with such power in these closing moments of the play is the excitement of a mind groping toward the humanist vision of a long tradition of cultural achievement that can enrich the lives of individuals and the community if only it is tapped into:

Listen to me! I'm tellin' you that the world's bin growing for two thousand years and we hevn't noticed it. I'm telling you that we don't know what we are or where we come from. I'm telling you something's cut us off from the beginning. I'm telling you we've got no roots. Blimey Joe! We've all got large allotments, we all grow things around us so we should know about roots. You know how to keep your flowers alive don't you Mother? Jimmy—you know how to keep the roots of your veges strong and healthy. It's not only the corn that need strong roots, you know, it's us too. (148; 1:146)

Jacqueline Latham's analysis of the skill with which Wesker reconciles "the demand for realism in the dialogue with the need for ritual formality'' helps to account for the extraordinary theatrical impact of this concluding speech. Beatie's liberation through language is not a matter of her abandoning the way of talking that she shares with her community for Ronnie's more consciously cultivated discourse. ''Beatie speaks in the same manner as her mother would, though her sentiments are different.''[36] And even as she rises to her theme of being cut off from the roots that connect the present with two thousand years of cultural and social development, she is ironically unaware of the strength she draws from the family that is *''sitting down to eat''*—always a potent image of communal life in Wesker's theater—quite untouched by the significance of Beatie's victory as she *''stands alone, articulate at last''* (151; 1:148).

NOTES

1. The first presentation of the complete *Wesker Trilogy* was at the Royal Court Theatre, London, in June-July 1960. The individual plays were all premiered at the Belgrade Theatre, Coventry: *Chicken Soup with Barley* on 7 July 1958, *Roots* on 25 May 1959, and *I'm Talking about Jerusalem* on 28 March 1960. The original, shorter version of *The Kitchen*, written in 1956, was first presented at the Royal Court Theatre on 13 September 1959, and the full-length version at the same theater on 27 June 1961. *Chips with Everything* was first presented at the Royal Court Theatre on 27 April 1962.

2. Kenneth Tynan's review of *Look Back in Anger*, reprinted in *A View of the English Stage*, 177–78; A. R. Jones, ''The Theatre of Arnold Wesker,'' 369.

3. John Orr, *Tragic Drama and Modern Society: A Sociology of Dramatic Form from 1880 to the Present*, 265.

4. Henry Goodman, ''The New Dramatists: 2. Arnold Wesker,'' 216.

5. John Kershaw, *The Present Stage: New Directions in the Theatre Today*, 52; Katharine J. Worth, *Revolutions in Modern English Drama*, 36.

6. John Russell Brown, *Theatre Language: A Study of Arden, Osborne, Pinter and Wesker*, 159.

7. Laurence Kitchin, ''Playwright to Watch,'' 196.

51

8. Glenda Leeming and Simon Trussler, *The Plays of Arnold Wesker: An Assessment*, 26. Wesker specifies in his introduction to the text of *The Kitchen* that the waitresses are to carry empty plates and that the activities of the cooks are to be mimed throughout.

9. Ronald Hayman, "Second Interview," in *Arnold Wesker*, 92.

10. Michael Anderson, "Arnold Wesker: The Last Humanist?" 11.

11. Hayman, "Second Interview," in *Arnold Wesker*, 15.

12. Leeming and Trussler, *Plays*, 31.

13. Wesker records that the interlude was added at the suggestion of the play's first director, John Dexter, who felt that it needed a quiet middle section. See Ronald Hayman, "Arnold Wesker and John Dexter," 90.

14. For a study of the place of ritual in Wesker's work see Thomas P. Adler, "*The Wesker Trilogy* Revisited: Games to Compensate for the Inadequacy of Words."

15. Laurence Kitchin, "Drama With a Message: Arnold Wesker," 179.

16. Peter's frustration includes his quarrelsome affair with the married waitress, Monique, but the sexual dimension of his predicament is not where Wesker lays the thematic emphasis.

17. *Roots*, unlike the other plays of the Trilogy, has been widely performed by repertory companies and amateur dramatic societies in Britain and was successfully revived by the National Theatre Company in 1979 and 1988. It has also been a popular text with school examination boards. For an account of provincial Beaties, see Glenda Leeming, *Wesker the Playwright*, 51–52.

18. Anderson, "Arnold Wesker," 15.

19. Ibid., 15.

20. Brown points out that the name "Ronald" (like the later "Roland" in *The Friends*) is an anagram of "Arnold" and that both characters bear "close resemblances" to their creator "in experience and opinion" (*Theatre Language*, 186–87).

21. Wesker explained in an interview with Simon Trussler that he did not set out with the plan of writing three linked plays, "Half-way through *Roots*, when I knew I wanted to write *Jerusalem*, it occurred to me that the three plays formed a trilogy" ("His Very Own and Golden City," 82).

22. Wesker, "Fears of Fragmentation" (October 1968), reprinted in *Fears of Fragmentation*, 113.

23. Hayman, "Second Interview," in *Arnold Wesker*, 93.

24. Of all the characters in the Trilogy, Dobson is the one who most blatantly embodies an argument that Wesker wants to find a voice for. Whereas Dave's experiment is in the spirit of William Morris, Dobson tried to put into practice the ideas of another nineteenth-century socialist, Robert

Owen, by founding a chain of garages owned by the mechanics who worked in them.

25. Martin Esslin, *The Theatre of the Absurd,* rev. ed. (Harmondsworth: Penguin, 1968), 24, 26.

26. Samuel Beckett, *Proust and Three Dialogues* (London: Calder and Boyars, 1970), 13, 64.

27. Quoted by Esslin, 127.

28. Laurence Kitchin, for example, has written that the first act "establishes the first authentic rural community since the Tudor drama which I, for one, had yet seen on the English stage" (*Mid-Century Drama,* 112).

29. John Russell Brown has noted that, in contrast to the silences in plays by Pinter or Osborne, "Here silences are usually corporate, and indications of personal and social limitations rather than clues to hidden power or tension" (*Theatre Language,* 164).

30. Quoted by Catherine Itzin, *Stages in the Revolution: Political Theatre in Britain Since 1968,* 104. In an early attack on Wesker's views on art, John Garforth dismissed him as one of those "well-intentioned middle-class idealists" who have mistakenly tried to impose their "own culture and values" on their working-class audience. See "Arnold Wesker's Mission," 229.

31. Quoted in Itzin, *Stages in the Revolution,* 105, from unpublished correspondence between Wesker and McGrath.

32. Tom Costello, "The Defeat of Naturalism in Arnold Wesker's *Roots,*" 40.

33. Kershaw, *The Present Stage,* 48.

34. Costello, "The Defeat of Naturalism," 40–41.

35. Jacqueline Latham, "*Roots:* A Reassessment," 195, 193.

36. Ibid., 195–97.

CHAPTER THREE

Rebels and Revolutionaries:

Chips with Everything, Their Very Own and
Golden City, **and** *The Friends*

Reflecting at the beginning of a new decade on the lessons
he had learned from the writing and reception of the Trilogy,
Wesker hinted that his way forward as a dramatist "might be
away from naturalism."[1] He later reported that the recently
completed draft of *Chips with Everything* was the result of "a
desperate bid to tear away from the conventions," but he was
also careful to head off any suspicion that he might be flirting
with formal experimentation for its own sake, "I have always
said, right from the beginning, that if I have any importance
at all, it is not because of my style, but because of what I am
saying." Indeed, he went further and confessed that "art is
beginning to have no meaning for me—it is not enough. . . .
I suppose this is one of the reasons why I will be sitting down
outside the Ministry of Defence—one is at a loss to do anything any more, except acts like that."[2] Political gestures of
this kind were not enough for Wesker the committed writer,
however, and *Chips with Everything* marks the point at which
he decided to suspend his career as a playwright in order to
do something practical about the gulf that separated the
working-class artist from the potential working-class audience. Like Dave Simmonds in *I'm Talking about Jerusalem,*
Wesker had come to feel that he had "talked enough." Or, as

he put it in an article about the early days of Centre 42 in March 1962, "Is it my responsibility as an artist only to analyse and complain?"[3] His answer was not to turn away from an unsatisfactory society in search of personal salvation, like Dave and Ada, but to commit himself to the task of transforming the cultural landscape of the materially affluent Britain of the 1960s. The three plays to be discussed in this chapter can be read as a prologue, an allegorical counterpart, and an epilogue to that endeavor.

Chips with Everything (1962)

Chips with Everything opened at the Royal Court Theatre on 27 April 1962. There was some adverse response to the elements of stylization in language and structure from reviewers who had Wesker firmly stereotyped as a social realist, but the play's emotional power and dazzling theatrical effects had enough popular appeal for it to transfer to the West End. It was hailed by Harold Hobson as "the left-wing drama's first real breakthrough, the first anti-Establishment play of which the Establishment has cause to be afraid."[4] Such a claim could be made because Wesker had discovered in the rigid hierarchical structure of service life not only a convenient microcosm of the English class system but also a vehicle for dramatizing both the processes by which one class keeps another in subjection and the possibility of resistance. *The Kitchen* had exposed the effects of capitalism on a group of workers—exploiting their labor, stunting their dreams, and generating an isolated and futile act of sabotage. The plays about the Kahn and Simmonds families had charted the disillusionment of two generations of working-class idealists in the face of political betrayal and the power of an industrialized economy. The victory celebrated in *Roots* had been confined to the awakening of one working-class spirit to the nature and causes of cultural oppression: "The whole stinkin' commercial world insults us and we don't care a damn" (150; 1:148). Wesker's move from the family settings of the Trilogy to the public context of the class struggle in *Chips with Everything* is signalled by Corporal Hill's opening address to the new batch of recruits, "Right, you're in the R.A.F. now, you're not at home" (12; 3:14).

Nevertheless, although he is concerned with the representative and politically significant aspects of what happens to one set of working-class conscripts billeted together during the eight weeks of basic training, he does not lose sight of the personal dimension of their lives, both as individuals and as a group. It was the greater complexity of the task he had set himself that created the need to "tear away from the conventions" of the Trilogy and to experiment with an episodic structure and techniques of caricature and stylization. The result is a play that is much more artfully constructed and that has much greater variety of pace and style than Wesker's earlier slices of social realism. Dramatic attention is switched skillfully from the easy naturalism of banter among off-duty airmen to the heightened monologues of Pip and Smiler, from the deliberately stylized verbal routines with which Corporal Hill establishes discipline on the parade ground to the more literary parodies of service rhetoric devised for the officers in the lecture hall, from the aggressive confrontations between authority and the wayward individual to the more intimate intensity of the duologues between Pip and Chas. Many of the scenes have an illustrative and freestanding quality, which has led some critics to invoke the name of Brecht,[5] but careful juxtapositioning of one scene with another and a tight control of the overall structure release significances that reach beyond the single episode.

The first four scenes of act 1 economically establish the nature and purpose of the period of basic training that supplies Wesker with the raw material for both the documentary and the metaphorical aspects of the play. Corporal Hill's intimidating harangue in scene 1 is evidently a well-rehearsed performance in which he presents himself as the embodiment of a system that subordinates personality to conditioning: "My name is Corporal Hill. I'm not a very happy man, I don't know why. I never smile and I never joke—you'll soon see that. Perhaps it's my nature, perhaps it's the way I've been brought up—I don't know. The R.A.F. brought me up" (12; 3:14). Anonymity is deliberately imposed upon the new recruits. They are addressed as an impersonal group and distinguished only by age and size; the two oldest are appointed "senior man" and "assistant" in the hut, and the two smallest are charged with doing odd jobs for the corporal. Scene 2, set in the canteen, allows a glimpse of the individuality denied them in scene 1. Wilfe sings an ironic plea for rescue to his mother; Chas reminisces about the two girls he has left "at home"; Ginger looks forward to his wedding; and Pip reveals that he is "scorching rich," with a banker father who used to be a general. The flurry of antagonism provoked by Pip's upper-class accent leads into his poetic reverie about the experience in an East End café that opened his eyes to the gulf between his own privileged background and the tastes and expectations shared by his fellow conscripts, "You breed babies and you eat chips with everything" (16; 3:17). In the next scene, Corporal Hill begins the process of shaping this motley collection of individuals into an efficient marching machine; and in scene 4, the physical drill of the parade ground is complemented by the ideological drill of the lecture hall, which exposes the values and methods of representative members of the ruling caste to satirical scrutiny by means of caricature: the Wing Commander, ''A Meteor, fully armed, is more important than a library''; the Squadron Leader, ''You are here to learn discipline''; the Pilot Officer, ''I want a man clean from toe nail to hair root. I want him so clean that he looks unreal. In fact I don't want real men, real men are dirty and nasty. . . . '' (21–23; 3:21–23).

The seeds of future dramatic action and symbolic symmetry are also sown in this introductory movement of the play, with the hint of a rift between Pip and his father and the picking out of two recruits who will not be amenable to service discipline—Smiler, because of an involuntary facial expression that annoys the corporal, ''You, I said wipe off that smile'' (19; 3:20); and Pip, because of a scarcely concealed contempt for the Wing Commander, ''There's insolence in those eyes, lad . . . take that glint out of your eyes, your posh tones don't fool me'' (21; 3:21). The doomed relationship that Pip and Chas will attempt to build across the class divide and Pip's open defiance of authority are also implicit in the exchange of social and personal challenges that closes scene 4:

> PIP: You have babies, you eat chips and you take orders.
> CHAS: Well, look at you then, I don't see you doing different. (24; 3:23)

In the next pair of scenes, the Pilot Officer makes awkward overtures of friendship toward one of the young airmen; and Pip, having captivated Chas's imagination with a tale about one of his ancestors, spurns his eager request for "more stories" with a dismissive, "What's the use?" There is no easy escape from the effects of social conditioning, and Pip will prove to have far more in common with the Pilot Officer than with his working-class comrade in the ranks—a bitter outcome that is foreshadowed in the Pilot Officer's warning, "We slum for our own convenience" (26; 3:25). Scene 6 also sees the burgeoning of a sense of communal identity among the inmates of the hut, as they settle down to the evening chores of cleaning shoes and brasses and writing letters while a more relaxed and paternal Corporal Hill plays his mouth organ in response to Ginger's, "Give us a good tune, Corp, go on" (32; 3:30).

Everything is now set for the first climax of the action at the Christmas Eve party in the Naafi, where the Wing Commander's plan to trick the conscripts into betraying the cultural poverty of the "good old working class of England" with a "dirty recitation, or a pop song" is thwarted when Pip persuades Andrew to recite a Scottish ballad about the birth of Christ and mobilizes the entire group in an aggressive rendering of an old peasant revolt song. This stirring assertion of collective dignity and class solidarity is complicated as a theatrical experience because, ironically, of its inception and orchestration by a defector from the camp of the class enemy. It is an open question how far Pip is genuinely concerned about his working-class companions and how far he is pursuing more personal ends, as Andrew shrewdly suspects,

"If you have a war with that man, Pip, don't use me as fodder, I'm warning you" (36; 3:34).

The remainder of act 1 develops further the feeling of community among the men in Hill's hut and Pip's relationships with the group as a whole and with Chas in particular. In the longest and most intimate duologue of the play, which provides an interlude of quiet after the climactic singing of "The Cutty Wren" and the acrimonious breakup of the party, Pip and Chas attempt to negotiate the difficulties that stand in the way of genuine friendship between human beings from different ends of the social and educational spectrum. Back in the sanctuary of the warm hut, Hill finds solace in his music, while Pip joins Smiler, Chas, and Dickey in a game of cards, Dodger distributes chocolate from his uncle's sweet shop, and Ginger and Cannibal dream of the useful trades they will learn in the RAF once their basic training is completed. Andrew articulates the nature of the atmosphere that Wesker has so deftly created in scene 9—one of those moments of harmony that offers consolation and hope to the human spirit: "I like us. All of us, here now. I like us all being together here. In a way you know I don't mind it, anything. Old Corp and his mouth-organ—all of us, just as we are, I like us" (47; 3:44). Ginger's announcement, "We've run out of coke you know," prompts the celebrated raid on the coke store, which ironically marks Pip's acceptance as a member of the community at the same time as elevating him to a position of leadership. Pip's own ambivalence is indicated by an uncertain use of pronouns—now merging his identity with that of the group ("Think we can't outwit them?") and now dissociating himself both from his own class and from that of his companions ("If you can't outwit them for a lump of coke,

then they deserve to have you in here for a couple of years''
[47–48; 3:44]). After the suspense and exhilaration of a scene
that has to be *"silent, precise, breathtaking, and finally very
funny,"* the first act ends on a subdued note, with Pip's bitter
denunciation of the corporal's unthinking deference to the
system, a bitterness provoked by a reluctant acknowledgment
that the point Hill makes in the following dialogue has just
been illustrated by Pip's own role in the coke-stealing exploit:

> HILL: You always need leaders.
> PIP [*ironically*]: Always!
> HILL: Well, don't you always need leaders?
> PIP: Always, always!
> HILL: Yes, always, always?
> PIP: Always, always, always! Your great-great-grand-
> father said there'll always be horses, your great-
> grandfather said there'll always be slaves, your grand-
> father said there'll always be poverty and your father
> said there'll always be wars. Each time you say "al-
> ways" the world takes two steps backwards and stops
> bothering. And so it should, my God, so it should—
> (50; 3:46–47)

The narrative of act 2 is structured by the contrasting and
converging careers of the play's two outsiders. The first three
scenes trace the path of Smiler from hut to parade ground to
guardhouse, where his slovenliness and incompetence are re-
viled by the noncommissioned officers responsible for turning
him into an efficient serviceman, "We'll break you, Smiler,
we'll break you, because that's our job" (57; 3:52). The next
five scenes follow the course of Pip's deliberate rebellion
against the RAF and the class that controls it: his insistence

61

that he will not apply for officer training and his refusal to take part in the degrading barbarity of bayonet practice; a brief dialogue with Andrew, which effects Pip's isolation from the other recruits—"No one's asking you to make gestures on our behalf. . . . The boys will hate any heroic gesture you make" (63; 3:58); his moral capitulation in a one-to-one confrontation with the Pilot Officer; and his symbolic submission to the system as he obeys Corporal Hill's order and *"rushes at the dummy, sticking it three times, with three screams"* (66; 3:60). In scene 9, a demoralized Pip rebuffs Chas's urgent appeals for the intellectual stimulation of his friendship and is in turn branded as a hypocrite and a "lousy word-user" by the man in whom he has aroused an appetite for knowledge. Chas's personal disappointment is accompanied by a resurgence of class resentment, "Your bleedin' stuffed grandfathers kept us stupid all this time, and now you come along with your pretty words and tell us to fend for ourselves" (68; 3:62). Smiler's abortive attempt to desert, distilled into the soliloquy of scene 10, interrupts these painful recriminations, and his exhausted and pitiful figure becomes the dramatic focus for the various resolutions of scene 11. Chas prevents Pip from ministering to the runaway's bleeding feet—"Leave him. I'll do it"—and Pip is excluded from the symbolic ceremony of brotherhood when the other men return from the Naafi: *"As many as possible manoeuvre SMILER so that his jacket and trousers come off, with the least disturbance. This action is done lovingly and with a sort of ritual"* (72; 3:66). It is Chas who initiates the group's resistance when the Pilot Officer orders Corporal Hill to take Smiler to the guardroom, but it is Pip who intervenes and, after a knowing exchange of smiles with the Pilot Officer, assumes both the uniform and the authority of the officer class in order to save his former mates from punishment. This time, the shifting reference of Pip's pronouns charts the gradual merging of his self-image with the social stance inherited from his class, as he adopts the patronizing tone of those born to rule:

> I suggest, sir, that you don't touch one of them. . . . We won't let him will we Charles—because you're right. Smiler has been badly treated and you are right to protect him. It's a good virtue that, loyalty. You are to be commended, Charles, all of you; it was a brave thing to do, protect a friend. We lack this virtue all too often, don't you agree, sir? These are good men, sometimes we are a little hasty in judging them—don't you agree, sir, a little too hasty? . . . We like you for it, we're proud of you, happy with you—you do agree, don't you, sir? These are the men we need and these are the men we must keep. (72–73; 3:66–67)

The public ceremony of the passing-out parade that closes the play—"Slope that rifle, stiffen that arm—I want to see them all pointing one way, together—unity, unity"—is in ironic counterpoint to the private ritual that bound the conscripts together in human sympathy for their stricken comrade in the previous scene. And the Wing Commander's satisfaction—"you have turned out well, as we expected, nothing else would have done, just as we expected" (74; 3:68)—cannot quite eradicate the memory of the challenge to the smug security of the ruling caste that flared up momentarily in defense of Smiler. Chas, the instigator of that challenge, has become aware of the need to broaden his intellectual horizons, as Beatie did under the influence of Ronnie, and has taken the first tentative step toward political action in the face of injustice and inhumanity. On this occasion, the system has easily absorbed his gesture of dissent, as the bland confidence of the Pilot Officer had absorbed Pip's more selfishly motivated revolt against the arrogance of his father's world: "We listen but we do not hear, we befriend but do not touch you, we applaud but we do not act. To tolerate is to ignore" (60; 3:56). Pip's rebellion collapses when its psychological sources are exposed by the Pilot Officer, who functions very much as his alter ego throughout the play: "Shall I say it? Shall I? Power. Power, isn't it? Among your own people there were too many who were powerful, the competition was too great, but here, among lesser men—here among the yobs, among the good-natured yobs, you could be king. . . . No man survives whose motive is discovered, no man" (65; 3:59–60). As the character at the center of the play's narrative, Pip Thompson is a complex study of the socially privileged rebel disabled by a lack of genuine and disinterested respect—what Sarah Kahn called simply "love"—for those whom he theoretically seeks to serve. Nearer to the heart of Wesker's hope for the future, however, is the potential activist from the ranks of the oppressed, who might inspire others to demand justice and the right to improve their own situation. In Wesker's next major play, the roles of Pip and Chas are conflated in the figure of Andrew Cobham, an architect from a working-class background who manages to infiltrate both the British establishment, by way of his profession, and the Labour movement, with a radical scheme for transforming the quality of life of the underprivileged masses, only to find himself forced to surrender to its values as the price of partial success.[6]

Their Very Own and Golden City (1965)

Wesker apparently began work on *Their Very Own and Golden City* in 1963, some eighteen months after he had announced that the Centre 42 project would require all his attention in the early stages of its development.[7] The new play, completed during 1964, failed in the British production at the Royal Court Theatre in 1966, partly because its political message was felt to be too overt and too earnest and partly because the director, William Gaskill, lacked the sympathetic insight into Wesker's combination of intellectual argument and human warmth that John Dexter had brought to the earlier plays. A revised version was performed with much greater success under the author's own direction at the Municipal Theater in Aarhus, Denmark, in May 1974.[8] Interviewed in February 1964, before he had finished the script, Wesker described it as "allegorical," "a development of or from *Chips*," and "certainly my most ambitious work—technically and intellectually."[9]

The premise on which the play's allegorical narrative rests is enunciated by the young Andy, as his spirit responds to the soaring architecture of Durham Cathedral in the opening scene: "Supposing you had the chance to build a city, a new one, all the money in the world, supposing that; this new city—what would you do with it? . . . The chance to change the pattern of living for all time?" (14; 2:130). This fantasy of a fresh start for society has its origins in the Jewish "dream of the millennium" and in certain brands of nineteenth-century socialism, as Heinz Zimmermann has pointed out:

> Wesker's writings blend inherited Messianism with social-
> ist utopia, in effect, Robert Owen's New Harmony with
> the Heavenly Jerusalem. This blending indicates the mys-
> tical source of energy from which this hope springs and
> also reveals the function of a utopian society for the au-
> thor: utopia replaces religion and creates new meaning.[10]

The *poetic* origin of the vision of "a liberated, enlightened secular society"[11] is made explicit by Andy himself in the second of the scenes in the cathedral with a quotation from "the prophet Blake": "Till we have built Jerusalem, dearly beloved apprentices, in England's green and pleasant land. Now, how can we build Jerusalem in England's green and pleasant land?" (33; 2:147).

In some respects, as Wesker acknowledged at the time,[12] his fictional protagonist's scheme to build six golden cities in which life-enhancing "gardens, concert halls, theatres, swimming pools" would displace the town hall from the vital heart of the community—"a rearrangement of priorities" (66; 2:176)—is derived from his own plans to "change the pattern of living" in contemporary Britain by promoting the foundation of a series of local arts and leisure centers. Certainly, some of the general features in the story of Andrew Cobham can be seen as directly parallel to Arnold Wesker's experiences as the initiator and artistic director of Centre 42. Both character and author, as artists from proletarian backgrounds, are fired by an idealistic mission to improve the quality of life among the working classes, and both come to recognize that "art is not enough"; both seek to enlist the active support of the Trades Union Congress for ambitious cultural schemes, and both eventually discover the harsh facts of political and economic life under a system in which capital and labor have learned to tolerate each other's existence. As one of the union leaders explains: "You didn't really expect them to vote in industry, you didn't really, did you? Private enterprise, let them do it, it's their job, not ours, Andy lad. Believe me, our own fights are enough" (85; 2:193). A more detailed mirroring of life in art might be detected in the parallel between Wesker's acquisition of the Round House as a base for Centre 42 and Andy's report that "after a year of searching, the first site for the first city has been found" (68; 2:178).

The quest for such identifications can be taken too far, however, in coming to terms with a play that is conceived essentially in a symbolic rather than a naturalistic mode. Some commentators, looking for social realism, have failed to adjust to the methods of the dramatic parable. Malcolm Page, for example, complains that act 2 is less firmly rooted in the actualities of postwar history and politics than the last act of *Chicken Soup with Barley* and *I'm Talking about Jerusalem*, "By giving so few specific details Wesker takes us into a shadowy world that has all too little connection with anywhere in the sixties."[13] Ronald Hayman also considers that the play does not succeed "in establishing itself as a valid image of our society," and he objects to the lack of specificity in its evocation of Andy's plans, so that "when we are told that the City has been built, we cannot altogether believe it. Because we cannot see it, even in our mind's eye.''[14] Wesker has countered this latter criticism by insisting that ''it's not a play about the rights and wrongs of a particular shape in a city,'' but about ''the spirit of the City, the relationships people have with each other which I see through the relationships people have with their work.''[15] An answer to the charge that the second half of the story does not adequately reflect the details of the political situation in Britain is partly implicit in the stage direction at the beginning of the long series of episodes that constitute the final scene: *''Covering the years 1948–90 or thereabouts.''*[16] Wesker's play undoubtedly grew out of his practical involvement with trades unionists and politicians in the early 1960s and his familiarity with the history of the Labour movement. (After all, its epigraph is taken from a lecture on Socialism given by William Morris in 1886, and the speeches of George Lansbury, the pacifist Labour statesman of the 1930s, were the direct source for some of Jake Latham's arguments against rearmament in act 1, scene 11.[17]) Nevertheless, the real subject of *Their Very Own and Golden City* is not the particular problems of launching Centre 42 nor the repeated failure of the left to carry through radical Socialist policies when in government. It is the more universal human cost of the perennial clash between idealists with a utopian vision and what Andy calls a ''cheapskate dreariness, a dull caution that kills the spirit of all movements and betrays us all—from plumber to poet'' (52; 2:163). Before the play had been produced in Britain, Wesker was at pains to explain that the city of the title was ''a simple idea,'' which was not itself significant: ''What's important is the tools that the people find in order to try and make it work and the extent to which they don't make it work. And the forces, the pressures, that make them compromise on each step."[18] It was this subject—distilled from history and autobiography but not dependent on documentary accuracy for its truth to human experience—that led Wesker to develop further the nonnaturalistic techniques of *Chips with Everything*.

The most controversial of those techniques is what the printed text describes as "a 'flash-forward' (as opposed to 'flash-back')" (9; 2:124). This device ideally requires different actors for the roles of the adolescent Andy, his future wife, and his two working-class friends in the five scenes located in Durham Cathedral in 1926 and for the roles of the successful middle-class professionals they turn into during the rest of the action. Wesker himself believed that the play was "irretrievably flawed" after its failure in London, where "the director made the mistaken and crippling decision (with which I foolishly agreed) to have one set of actors play both old and young protagonists," but his faith was restored when the Danish production gave him the opportunity to cast it according to his original conception.[19] He discovered that the "flash-forward" can be made to work if the cathedral remains on stage throughout the performance, so that the future talked about by the youngsters is played out inside it. The return to 1926 twice in each act then affords a powerful dramatic realization of two contradictory perspectives on time as the matrix of human endeavor: time as linear progression and time as generational cycle. As Michael Anderson puts it, in a persuasive account of the play: "While the clock of history cannot be turned back, youth, maturity and age is a pattern that repeats itself in every individual. One man's past is another man's future."[20] This concept is demonstrated in the scenes between Andy and Jake Latham set in 1933, when the raw idealist asks the seasoned campaigner, "What could you teach me?" (24; 2:139), and in 1936, when the rising star of local politics ruthlessly defeats the veteran pacifist in a debate over the issue of principle versus the unity of the Labour movement. Jake Latham warns, "Be careful of your cities, that's what I'm saying. One day you're old and you say right things—but it's all too late; that's what I'm saying" (47; 2:159). The point is reinforced by the juxtaposition of the play's last two episodes. In one, an aged Sir Andrew Cobham is playing cards with members of the political and financial establishment to which he now belongs and tries to silence his guilty conscience in an insistent whisper to his wife, "They're good people, Jessie, all of them, you listen to me, good, good people" (89; 2:197). In the other, back in the cathedral that first inspired him more than sixty years before, Young Andy brings the play to its conclusion with a confident reply to a question from Young Jessie, "Aye—and people are good" (91; 2:199). In this way, the device of a double time scheme is instrumental in dramatizing that inescapable tension between idealism and disillusionment that lies at the heart of Wesker's theater.

In overall structure, *Their Very Own and Golden City* is similar to *Chips with Everything*, in spite of its much longer time span. Act 1 establishes the character of Andy and charts the early stages of his career, in which he qualifies as an architect, leaves the private firm that employed him as a draughtsman to work for the local council, makes the acquaintance of Jake Latham at a meeting of his trade union branch, becomes a town councillor in order to press for a more enlightened housing policy, postpones his plans with the approach of the Second World War, and in the immediate postwar period finally abandons his hope of achieving anything through the bureaucratic mechanism of local government: "Slum clearances? Patchwork! All over the country bits and pieces of patchwork. I've done it" (49; 2:161).[21] Act 2 dramatizes the challenge that Andy, like Pip, makes to the inherited structures of society with his scheme to circumvent the processes of capitalism and build his cities as a cooperative enterprise—"Participation! We'll involve them, a real community project, a real one!" (56; 2:167)—and the subsequent erosion of his principles by the unshakeable power of the political and economic system.

Another development from the technical resources of *Chips with Everything* is the overlapping or counterpointing of episodes, which not only facilitates the rapid narrative movement across the years but is also expressive of the subtle effects of time upon individual resolve and self-perception. For instance, Andy's eager anticipation of imaginative political advances at the end of the second scene in the cathedral—"And when the new Labour comes, who will they turn to to build their homes?"—is echoed in the disillusioned exclamation that opens the next scene, set nine years later in 1935, "New Labour! New Labour! We never learn, never!" (34; 2:148); his insistence that "I don't want to go into local politics—I'm an architect" is followed immediately by Paul's inquiry a year later, "Is he going to stand for council again?" (37–38; 2:151). Perhaps most striking in its dramatic force is Young Andy's inspiring metaphor of the International Labour Movement as a ship that "can span every ocean there is, every ocean, look, and reach all corners of the world"—broken off at the end of the cathedral scene in the middle of act 2 with the words, "It seems to me—someone has to tell them that . . . ''—which merges into his speech to the Trades Union Congress in 1948 at the start of the next scene: ''Someone has to say, 'Look, look at that ship, it's more than a raft, it has sails. The wind can catch those sails and the ship can span every ocean there is. It can span every ocean and reach all corners of the earth' '' (62; 2:172–73).

Thematically, too, there are continuities and developments that link *Their Very Own and Golden City* with Wesker's earlier work. As always, he refuses to simplify the public dimension of his narrative by divorcing it from issues of private life and personality. The domestic incidents in which Andy complains to his wife that a button is missing from his shirt or that the house is a mess are as much a part of the play's texture and meaning as the occasions on which he addresses meetings and negotiates with trades union officials and government ministers. Central to the scheme of Wesker's complex dramatic allegory is the contrast between the two women, Jessie and Kate, who are not conventional rivals as wife and mistress but rather extensions of the private and public aspects of Andy's personality. Like Pip, Andy is driven by an essentially egotistical imperative: he announces in the first scene, ''I know everything I want to do with my life'' (14; 2:130). Again like Pip, he shies away from close personal involvement with others: he significantly draws expressions of love from both Jessie and Kate but never makes an explicit emotional commitment to either of them. He eventually confesses to Kate and their two bridge partners: ''We don't really like people, do we? We just like the idea of ourselves liking people'' (90; 2:197). Unable to share Sarah Kahn's conviction that ''you have to start with love,'' he sets out on both his private and his public pilgrimages with a clear idea of what he intends to achieve—an idea crystallized into two symbolically related dreams: "I want six children from you, Jessie. One after another, six of them" (20; 2:135) and "Six Golden Cities" (59; 2:170). Jessie's role, as she bitterly reminds him after years of being made to feel foolish and marginal to his life-long obsession, has been "to be treated like a hired housekeeper instead of your wife" (82; 2:190). The role of Kate—the self-styled "classless woman" of aristocratic origins—is to inject the ruthlessness that Andy will need if his idealistic plans are to be realized in a world governed by political apathy and economic self-interest. It is Kate who in act 1 plants in his mind the thought of becoming a local councillor, and Kate, in the crucial scene at the beginning of act 2, who goads him out of his postwar despair and effectively sets him on the road toward a cooperative venture. Once the scheme is under way, she urges him to channel all his energy into his public mission at the expense of his domestic responsibilities, "I charge you again—your family is your family and your work is your work, and you have not the right, no right at all, to neglect a project involving so many for the sake of your own good life" (67; 2:176). It is Kate again who arranges for him to meet Maitland, the right-wing minister of town and country planning, and later, when the unions back out, engineers the joint financing of the city's industry by the Conservative government and the capitalist businessman, Harrington.

The other significant character for Andy's development as a man and as a public figure is Jake Latham. He recognizes in the thrusting young architect of 1933 the promise of something more substantial than the personally motivated gestures of a Pip Thompson, and in doing so formulates one of

Wesker's primary distinctions between different kinds of dissent:

> I've no time for rebels, they hate the past for what it didn't give them. The Labour Movement is choked with bad-mannered, arrogant little rebels who enjoy kicking stubborn parents in the teeth. Revolutionaries is what we want—they spend less time rebelling against what's past and give their energy to the vision ahead. (23–24; 2:138)

Even more important for the drama's dialectical structure, Jake represents lifelong fidelity to an ideal as a counterbalance to the youthful idealism of the cathedral scenes, which is born anew with each generation. The creed he imparts to Andy in private, repeated almost word for word from a platform a few scenes later, is one of the central statements of the play: "Defeat doesn't matter; in the long run all defeat is temporary. It doesn't matter about present generations but future ones always want to look back and know that someone was around acting on principle" (26; 2:141). Andy will admit at the end of the debate that his open opposition to Jake in the interests of party unity was an act of private betrayal as well as public compromise—the first of a series of retreats from principle that undermine both his domestic happiness and his professional integrity.

Another of Jake Latham's speeches reverberates through the play and through much of Wesker's work: "What holds a movement together? Any movement, not even a movement, a group of people, say, or a family, or a nation or a civilization? Something must" (22–23; 2:137–38). Andy offers an answer to Jake's question fifteen years later in his address to the Trades Union Congress. It is an answer that expresses the inspiration that drove Arnold Wesker himself into his prolonged struggle to find a practical response to that other question thrown up at the end of his first play, "What is there more?":

We know what holds men in a movement through all time—their visions. Visions, visions, visions! What else? To fight for a penny more an hour for standing at the lathe, our energies for only this? . . . But men have minds which some good God has given so we can tackle problems bigger than our daily needs, so we can dream. Who dares to tell us we've no right to dream? (63; 2:173)

At the end of the Trilogy, Dave Simmonds's verdict that "visions don't work" had elicited Ronnie's desperate plea to "behave as though they do—or else nothing will work." Andy confronts this dilemma at the very moment when he is persuading his friends to help him launch the Monday Meetings that will set his dream on the path to fulfillment:

If I decide to build those cities, then I'll forget they could ever have been regarded as patchwork, I'll ignore history. . . . The alternative is that complete revolution we all used to talk about, but today? Here? Now?—there's no situation that's revolutionary, is there? Face it, all of you. There—is—no—revolutionary—situation.
    [*ANDY challenges them all but there is silence.*]
Then let's begin.
In the way you build a city you build the habits of a way of life in that city—that's a fact. Six Golden Cities could lay the foundations of a new way of life for all society— that's a half-truth, one that we're going to perpetuate, with our fingers crossed. (59; 2:169–70)[22]

Zimmerman has noted that Wesker differs from previous utopian writers in attempting to confront the problem of *how* the dream of a better world is to be implemented. He adds, "In *tours de force,* the conclusions of his plays always try to resolve the contradiction between failure and belief in an endeavour which acknowledges that the ideal is impossible to attain and yet, in spite of all, must not be abandoned."[23] After the tragic resonance of the soliloquy in which Andy assesses his long life's achievement—"Patchwork! Bits and pieces of patchwork. Six cities, twelve cities, what difference. Oases in the desert, that the sun dries up" (89; 2:196)—and the bitter irony of his absorption into the Establishment in the symbolic game of bridge, underlined by Maitland's reminder, "You're my partner now you know" (90; 2:197), the final return to Durham Cathedral constitutes one of Wesker's most brilliant dramatic solutions to the problem of how to give full weight to the realities of an imperfect world while literally keeping open the possibility of escape into a better one. The three "ragged-arsed brothers" of 1926 form a human chariot and convey Jessie out of the darkening enclosure of the medieval building in triumph, proclaiming the faith of the young in the certainty of liberation from the past—"We knew the door was open" (91; 2:198).

The Friends (1970)

The Friends was first performed by the Stadsteater in Stockholm on 24 January 1970 and opened at the Round House on 19 May 1970. Both productions were directed by the author himself. Difficulties that arose between Wesker and his cast during rehearsals may have been partly responsible for the play's mixed reception in London, where admiration for the musical structure and the atmosphere created by the solid and graceful set was balanced by critical hostility to what some felt to be a surfeit of ideas inadequately digested into dramatic form.

In the scene in the cathedral midway through the first act of *Their Very Own and Golden City,* Young Andy speaks to his "ragged-arsed brothers" of the satisfaction of shared endeavor: "There's something about people getting together and doing things. . . . a group together, depending on each other, knowing what they want, knowing how to get it—" (32; 2:146). *The Friends* is about another group of idealists—all but one of them products of "the same art college, same warm northern city, same kind of labouring fathers and tight-lipped mothers" (33; 3:95)—who had set out to use their talents in the service of their class with just this youthful sense of purpose. Now, in early middle age,[24] their missionary enthusiasm has evaporated and they have lost interest in the chain of interior design shops through which they once planned to enhance the lives of people like "Crispin's driver father" and "Tessa's bricklaying brothers" (34; 3:95–96). They are gathered symbolically in the sickroom of one of their number, Esther, who is dying of leukemia; and her death brings to a climax the crisis of identity they are undergoing individually and collectively, a crisis summed up by Tessa: "We're none of us what we thought we were. It's so late now" (57; 3:115).

The time scheme is more concentrated than that in any of Wesker's previous plays except *The Kitchen,* and time itself has a different quality from the representative working day of that early piece of social realism or the symbolic year in which love is coaxed into life, flowers, and fades in the poetic fable of *The Four Seasons.*[25] In this intense, introverted, and claustrophobic drama, the movement from afternoon, through the long hours of the deathwatch, to the cold light of morning constitutes a secular version of the dark night of the soul—a traumatic experience of disintegration, spiritual stock taking, and possible resolution.

There is very little in the way of narrative plot. Esther's death in the final moments of act 1 is the central event of the play, and there are eruptions of violence from time to time—when Roland cuts his body with a razor in a desperate attempt to share the pain of the woman he loves or when Tessa smashes her guitar to pieces in the anger of grief. Most of the activity on stage, however, is part of that physical texture of living that is so characteristic a feature of a Wesker play: Esther works on a mosaic of old photographs and is helped to walk around the room; Manfred, her brother, reads and makes notes or adds to a half-constructed model of the DNA molecule that stands near his desk; Crispin, another of the partners in the firm, fiddles intermittently with a toy he is designing; Roland attends to Esther's blankets or sits on the floor in a Yoga posture; Simone massages and bathes Tessa's feet; Tessa strums her guitar. But above all, on this night of self-confrontation and exorcism, the characters talk. They unfold their secret fears and shames in the pattern of interweaving conversations, duologues, and monologues that comprises the "condensed and involuted substance"[26] of this painfully introspective drama. The method is often reminiscent of Chekhov, as Margery Morgan suggests: "The characters pursue their separate trains of thought aloud, so that the lines intersect, or brush past each other without fully engaging."[27]

Coherence is to be looked for not in the evolution of an external action but in emotional rhythms and thematic structures. Wesker himself noted of the play's composition, ''I wanted to write it like a symphony.''[28]

The classical restraint of the single location and the brief time span, however, which is so different from the expansiveness of the Trilogy or *Their Very Own and Golden City,* has more than merely formal significance. Monica Mannheimer comments: ''The static setting heightens the sense of collective claustrophobia; the inexorable passing of the hours becomes a threat, as the arrival of morning indicates the futility of escapism and the necessity to come to terms with everyday life.''[29] For all its musical qualities and its lack of narrative interest, this play is above all the enactment of a significant moral action. Consequently its physical setting, in spite of the plethora of furniture and properties that might seem to recall Wesker's earlier naturalism, does not function in the same way as the sets of *The Kitchen* or *Roots.* The frenetic work place of Peter and his fellow cooks and the domestic interiors of the Beales' ramshackle house and the Bryants' tied cottage were felt as manifestations of an inhuman and unjust society that exerted an insidiously stultifying influence on the imaginations of its less privileged members. In contrast, the richly appointed room in which Esther is dying symbolizes not the determining effects of environment but the greater freedom to control their own lives that has resulted from the group's talents and education. As the drama unfolds, it becomes apparent that the value of the room and its openness to more than one interpretation are among the dominant issues of the play—for the characters no less than for the audience. Mannheimer recognizes that the ''main line of tension'' derives from an uncertainty about the outcome of the contest between Esther's "joyous acceptance of life" and "the paralysing fixation on life's agony and confusion" displayed by her companions; and Peter Bowering associates this contest directly with the set: "The room is Esther's; to her it is quiet and friendly, and the friends' subsequent attempt to disown the room and what it stands for becomes a rejection of both Esther and the values she embodies."[30]

The characters' own identification of the room with the lives they have created for themselves is made explicit early in the first scene:

> ROLAND: We're such an odious lot, us; not noble at all. No, no—majesty.
> CRISPIN: Like this room. No majesty here. Dishonest, that's what it is. We own five shops selling twentieth-century interiors which we've designed, *we've* designed, mind you, and yet look at this room. Bits and pieces from other men's decades. (15; 3:80)

Much later, after Esther's death, it is Tessa who articulates most lucidly the fear that possessions painstakingly assembled over a lifetime—including experiences and ideas—can become a cage from which there seems to be no way out: "I can't bear this room any more. We've built too much of ourselves into it. . . . And now we're trapped, hung up by it all. Bits and pieces of us all over the place" (66; 3:122). One of those "bits and pieces" takes on particular importance. In act 1, Tessa exhibits an unexplained hostility toward an eighteenth-century antique, whereas Simone points it out admiringly to Macey, the manager of the main shop and the only representative of an older generation, who has arrived with news of the imminent collapse of the business. In the final scene, this chair provides the focus for an ideological showdown between the two women. Tessa throws it to the ground in angry denunciation of the false values they have lived by: "Look at this room, look at the lovely order we've cluttered ourselves with. Dead and ancient riches, PER-FECT!"; and Simone *"rushes to pick it up, lovingly,"* and defends the room and the principles it enshrines: "You should love it. . . . Memory, the past, signs of human activity—you should cherish them—I adore this room" (66; 3:122).

This exchange between Tessa and Simone highlights one of the central themes of *The Friends,* which Wesker himself has formulated elsewhere as "the theme of the past's inexorable tie with the present—not its stranglehold but its fertilizing qualities."[31] Tessa shares with Manfred and Crispin a revulsion against the room because it witnesses to a reverence for continuity—what Beatie Bryant called "roots"—which for them stands in the way of necessary social change. But Simone inherits the vision of the life-loving Esther, whose last major speech develops the distinction made by Jake Latham in *Their Very Own and Golden City:*

> My brother's a rebel, Macey, I—am a revolutionary. He talks about leaders of our time, I see a need for men who belong to the end of a long line of all time. He's obsessed with our responsibility to the twentieth century, I'm obsessed with our responsibility to an accumulation of twenty centuries of sensibility. My brother is a rebel because he hates the past, I'm a revolutionary because I see the past as too rich with human suffering and achievement to be dismissed. (46; 3:106)

Jake, handing on the baton of idealism to the next generation, had stressed the need for revolutionaries to "give their energy to the vision ahead." For Esther, the overriding priority is to keep faith with what is valuable in the past. This shift of emphasis reflects Wesker's preoccupation during the period of the play's composition with a widespread cultural malaise that informs Tessa's ambivalent rejection of "the lovely order" that Esther has created around herself.[32] He speaks of it in a lecture delivered in October 1968 as the "fragmentation of vision" and defines it as the habit of elevating partial truths into universal theories in a desperate attempt to make personal sense of an increasingly complex and unstable universe. For example, fired by such a "fragment of the truth" as the socialist insight that a "competitive society is an evil one," there is a danger that well-intentioned reformers will "jettison everything from the old society because the labour of sorting out what is of value and what is worthless is too arduous."[33] Tessa is performing precisely this act in her blanket condemnation of Esther's room as a repository of "dead and ancient riches."

Wesker explains in the same lecture that his conception of art springs directly from his "fears of fragmentation" and from his awareness of the impossibility of satisfying the human hunger to "place everything in its inevitable order": "Yet this need to do so is, I think, the driving force behind all creative activity. The arrangement of fragments is the artist's purpose in life."[34] Esther is thus revealed to be the true artist as well as the true revolutionary of *The Friends* in her opening reverie, which takes the form of a recitation of things she has loved and valued—a spoken equivalent of the collage of old family photographs she is creating on a screen beside her bed and of her room itself: "Russian icons and pre-Raphaelites and Venetian chandeliers. . . . And Baroque churches and houses, fountains and market-places and the music of organs and Norman arches and wine and the cooking of friends and the sound of friends" (9–10; 3:75–76). It is as champion of this positive vision of human achievement through the ages that Simone, the outsider among the friends because of her more privileged background, finds her voice in the closing scene, much as Beatie did at the end of *Roots*.

The debate at the heart of *The Friends* is undeniably about specific cultural and political issues raised by Wesker's experiences as artistic director of Centre 42, a position from which he resigned later in the same year that the play received its British premiere in the Round House. Nevertheless, much of its somber dramatic power is drawn from an engagement with more fundamental fears and disappointments. The imminent death of one of their number forces each of the friends to confront the nature of the human condition and the ebbing away of youthful hope and purpose. Crispin is overwhelmed by man's potential for evil; Manfred panics at the relentless, disorienting flow of new scientific knowledge; Roland is conscious of personal loss of control— "That tight brain I had, all wrapped up with confidence—it's fallen apart" (56; 3:114); Simone and Macey share their bewilderment and distaste at the "sweet-natured grubbiness" of the "strange, young people" who are beginning to inherit the earth (28–29; 3:91–92); and Tessa faces a blank future— "What's left worth the while to do, Macey?" (59; 3:117)— and grimly sums up the situation of them all, "Esther's dead and suddenly we're old and we're none of us what we thought we were and that's not easy now, is it?'' (61; 3:118–19). Against this collective defeatism, Esther preaches the will to live:

> Some people of course know that when they're old they'll become tired and ready to go; or else they grow to despise themselves so much for not being what they thought they were that they become anxious and eager to fade out. Not me, though. Just not me. I can't tell you how much I cherish everything. . . . I want to stay on and not miss anything. (31–32; 3:94).

Simone's attempt to rally the friends from their despair is countered by Manfred's assertion that its causes lie deeper than grief at Esther's death and disillusionment over the collapse of their joint cultural enterprise:

> Our mess is not only made of Esther's dying, but the knowledge that this is a once and only life more than half over, and if you want to thrash the gloom from us then you'd have to give us back youth and the strength not to despise ourselves. Not all your haranguing us to order political priorities can clear up such a mess as that. It can't be ignored, that one, not that one. (69–70; 3:125)

In response to this, Simone shouts, ''THAT'S NOT GOOD ENOUGH!'' and devises a ceremony of collective reconciliation and affirmation. Repeating the phrase, ''She wanted to live,'' she draws them one by one into renewed contact with Esther, encouraging them to enthrone her dead body on the symbolic eighteenth-century chair with her face turned resolutely toward a portrait of Lenin. Having been *''forced to accept the presence of the dead among them''* (71; 3:126), they return quietly to the everyday business of living, folding blankets and clearing away coffee cups and dirty ashtrays. Wesker has since explained that this macabre tableau was inspired by a Romanian folk custom in which the mourners at a funeral dance joyfully with the corpse, ''This struck me very powerfully as a manifestation of the desperate need that men have to survive the knowledge of death: they will create extraordinary rituals for themselves so that they can live more easily with it.''[35] Living with the knowledge of death was a theme that would continue to preoccupy him in the play with which he opened the next decade of his career as a writer.

NOTES

1. Wesker, ''Discovery,'' 17.

2. Wesker, ''Art is Not Enough,'' 192–93.

3. Wesker, ''The Secret Reins: 'Centre Fortytwo' '' (March 1962); reprinted in *Fears of Fragmentation,* 42.

4. Review by Harold Hobson in *Sunday Times,* reprinted in Glenda Leeming, ed., *Wesker on File,* 23.

5. See Michael Anderson, ''Arnold Wesker: The Last Humanist?'' 21; Ronald Hayman, *Arnold Wesker,* 51.

6. Wesker has described the figures of Pip and Chas as ''two sides of myself'' (Simon Trussler, ''His Very Own and Golden City,'' 90).

7. Ibid., 87

8. The first performance of the play was in French at the Belgian National Theater in 1965. Wesker pays tribute to the director, actors, and technicians of the Aarhus company in the 1980 preface to the revised Penguin edition of the play.

9. Walter Wager, ''Interview with Arnold Wesker,'' 224.

10. Heinz Zimmerman, ''Wesker and Utopia in the Sixties,'' 191. Zimmerman points out that Andrew's ''golden cities'' project ''resembles Robert Owen's Villages of Co-operation, or his New Harmony in Indiana. . . . The communities are conceived as a model, a germ from which a general revolutionary change is supposed to develop'' (197).

11. Ibid., 197.

12. Wesker speaks of "obvious parallels" in the interview with Trussler, "His Very Own and Golden City," 92.

13. Malcolm Page, "Whatever Happened to Arnold Wesker?: His Recent Plays," 324.

14. Ronald Hayman, *Arnold Wesker*, 61–62.

15. Hayman, "Second Interview" in *Arnold Wesker*, 101.

16. This is changed to "1948–85 or thereabouts" in the 1981/90 edition.

17. Some of Jake's words are "taken verbatim from Lansbury's speeches." See Hayman, *Arnold Wesker*, 65.

18. Interview with Giles Gordon, "Arnold Wesker: An Interview," 20.

19. See the preface to the 1981/90 Penguin edition.

20. Anderson, "Arnold Wesker," 22.

21. In the 1981/90 Penguin edition, Wesker changed the point at which the division between the acts occurs; in the earlier version, act 1 closes with the third scene in the cathedral; in the revised text, act 1 closes with the first postwar scene, so that act 2 opens with the crucial discussion between Kate and Andy, in which she goads him out of his sense of defeat.

22. In the original text, the end of this passage reads differently, "That's a lie, but that's the lie we're going to perpetuate, with our fingers crossed."

23. Zimmerman, "Wesker and Utopia," 192.

24. In the 1970 Cape edition, they are said to be *"between the ages of 35 and 38";* in the 1980/90 Penguin text, this has been changed to *"between the ages of 40 and 45."*

25. *The Four Seasons* was written after *Their Very Own and Golden City* but first produced before it on 24 August 1965 at the Belgrade Theatre in Coventry.

26. Glenda Leeming and Simon Trussler, *The Plays of Arnold Wesker: An Assessment,* 140.

27. Margery M. Morgan, "Arnold Wesker: The Celebratory Instinct," 38.

28. Garry O'Connor, "Production Casebook No. 2: Arnold Wesker's 'The Friends,' " 78.

29. Monica Mannheimer, "Major Themes in Arnold Wesker's Play *The Friends*," 112.

30. Mannheimer, "Major Themes," 112; Peter Bowering, "Wesker's Quest for Values," 72.

31. Wesker, "Casual Condemnations: A Brief Study of the Critic as Censor," 23.

32. Wesker has revealed that his first notes for the play are dated 12 June 1966, that he began writing it on 20 January 1967, and that he was still

adding notes to the written draft in June 1968. See Simon Trussler, Catherine Itzin and Glenda Leeming, ''A Sense of What Should Follow,'' 7. Monica Mannheimer has identified seven versions of the text between the original handwritten draft of January–September 1967 and the Cape edition of 1970 in ''Ordering Chaos: The Genesis of Arnold Wesker's *The Friends.*''

33. Wesker, ''Fears of Fragmentation'' (October 1968); reprinted in *Fears of Fragmentation,* 107.

34. Ibid., 106.

35. Trussler, Itzin and Leeming, ''A Sense of What Should Follow,'' 8.

CHAPTER FOUR

Coming to Terms:
The Old Ones, The Wedding Feast,
and *The Merchant/Shylock*

The 1970s proved to be a time of serious stock taking for Arnold Wesker—as an artist, as a political campaigner, and as a human being. After the generally unfavorable reception of *The Four Seasons* and *Their Very Own and Golden City* and the troubles that beset the London production of *The Friends*,[1] the new decade began hopefully with the prospect of reestablishing his position in the British theater with premières by the two major national companies. *The Old Ones,* written in 1970, was due to be directed by John Dexter at the National Theatre; *The Journalists,* set in the offices of a Sunday newspaper and conceived (like *The Kitchen*) as an orchestration of the corporate activity of human beings at work, was scheduled for performance by the Royal Shakespeare Company in October 1972. Neither project actually came to fruition. Angered by a decision to postpone the production of *The Old Ones,* Dexter took the play to the Royal Court Theatre, where it was first performed on 8 August 1972, to the ultimate satisfaction of neither author nor director.[2] The fate of *The Journalists* was even more discouraging. Many of the actors disliked the roles offered to them, and the subsequent abandonment of the play led to a lengthy legal controversy between the dramatist and the company.[3] In spite of these setbacks, Wesker went on to write four more plays during the 1970s, only one of which—*Love Letters on Blue Paper*—was produced in London. The last—*One More Ride on the Merry-go-round*—remained unperformed until 1985, when it was produced at the Phoenix Theatre in Leicester. The other two—*The Wedding Feast* and *The Merchant*—were premiered overseas and given their first British productions in the provincial cities of Leeds and Birmingham.

It is not surprising that as the decade wore on, Wesker was feeling increasingly neglected in his own country, whatever his acclaim abroad, and was seeking reasons for his failure to sustain the reputation earned by the early plays and for the mixture of incomprehension and hostility with which his later work had been greeted. One explanation was that the uplifting experience of Beatie's victory at the end of *Roots* had created expectations that were bound to be disappointed, "In a strange way I think that all the other plays have been incorrectly seen through the rose glasses of this one play."[4] Another, which Wesker put forward during a symposium on contemporary playwriting, was that he no longer fitted comfortably into the theatrical environment that had emerged in Britain since 1968, "I feel very much between two camps now. I had a moment of feeling that I was in among the establishment—but there are two kinds of establishment now, there's the fringe-establishment and the establishment-establishment, and I find myself falling between the two."[5]

On the political front, the collapse of Centre 42 was only one factor in Wesker's growing dismay at the cultural condition of British society and his reluctant acknowledgment that there are irreconcilable contradictions at the heart of socialism. One strand in the development of his thinking can be traced in the changes made to a passage in *Love Letters on Blue Paper* during its adaptation from a short story published in 1974 to a stage play performed in 1977. In the earlier version, Victor, a former Trades Union leader dying of leukemia, speaks despairingly to a friend about the attitude of a young union official who is more interested in securing "power and affluence" than in the moral and social justice of his cause: "Can't win now, Maurice, capitalism's built up a resistance to criticism. Like certain diseases, all the known antibiotics can't touch them."[6] The dramatized version shifts the emphasis from the resilience of the capitalist system to the failure of socialism to supply a worthy alternative, "Capitalism has created an enemy in its own image, monstrous as itself" (3:224). In an interview given when he was working on another story, "The Visit," Wesker explained that he shared his characters' bewilderment when confronted by "the conflict between the social nature of co-operation in a socialist society, and the anti-social nature of state control."[7] A family holiday in Eastern Europe in 1977 had left him troubled by the contrast between "the death of the human spirit" and the "terrible social listlessness" in East Berlin and the "energy . . . which made one feel the people were alive and human" in West Berlin, "with all its vulgarity, its cheapness, with all the things I actually don't like and in Western society criticize."[8] In the following autumn, Catherine Itzin reported that this and other recent experiences had left the dramatist feeling isolated and powerless, "Wesker now felt that his energy for public, political life had been expended."[9]

Along with a sense of his own marginal position as an artist and deepening doubts about the viability of political solutions to the cultural sickness of his society went an urgent need to come to terms with the biological and moral dimensions of the human condition. A paragraph in a private journal dated August 1969 touches on themes that were to be explored in a variety of ways in the drama and prose stories of the next ten years:

Growing old involves being able to cope less and less with those human faults whose inevitability one had always suspected while still young but had ignored. The sadness of it. Of the greed in men and the fear they need to inflict in order to protect their own miserable self-hates. Growing old is not a losing of faith—no point in losing that, there's too much goodness. No, ageing involves being less cheered by goodness than one is tormented by evil. [10]

In 1978, in *One More Ride on the Merry-go-round,* in a speech of self-justification by an academic on the verge of age fifty who has just resigned from his university post, Wesker made a slight but telling adjustment to the phrasing he had used ten years earlier: ''I'm not old but I'm older than I'm younger, and though I love life I'm not too impressed with the living. Man's goodness cheers me too little to remain untormented by his stupidity'' (6:16).

This apparent drift toward exhaustion and despair, however, is only one side of Wesker's evolution during the decade following the demise of Centre 42. Characteristically, he responded to the almost universally scathing reviews of *The Friends* with a long and reasoned examination of the damaging effects of ill-considered criticism not only upon the self-confidence of the individual writer but also upon the freedom to experiment in the art of theater. [11] The savage treatment meted out to *The Old Ones* goaded him into a series of shorter replies, in which he complained of "the slow evaporation of standards in dramatic art-criticism"[12] and took the reviewers to task for "private spites, ill-will, carelessness and the specially journalistic ego."[13] *The Journalists* was conceived as part of this campaign of self-defense against the "journalistic ego" in the wake of the hostility aroused by Centre 42 and the London production of *The Friends,* "The idea for the play came to me after I became aware of the degree to which I found my own zest for work, public actions, and myself had become eroded by reviews, journalistic profiles, and columnists' attacks."[14] The journalist at the center of the play's main narrative embodies what Wesker has defined elsewhere as "the Lilliputian mentality," which "diminishes or minimalizes" the achievements of others by its mean-spirited assumption "that success is accompanied by smugness and complacency."[15] Toward the end, her editor points out the dangers inherent in an irresponsible use of·the power of the press, "You might want to deflate the egos of self-styled 'gods' but be careful you don't crack the confidence of good men" (122; 4:92).

Wesker's own confidence may have been temporarily shaken by the reviewers and by the actors' rejection of *The Journalists,* but the vigor of his imagination and his theatrical inventiveness remained unimpaired during the 1970s.

The Old Ones (1972)

In October 1969, while he was preparing to go to Stockholm to direct the world premiere of *The Friends,* Wesker made a significant entry in a week-long diary commissioned by Swedish Radio: "It seems I've little patience these days for work that is anecdotal. There seems such little time left for stories. . . . Broad surfaces no longer hold me. I must go deeper into smaller areas."[16] The results of this determination are evident in both *The Friends* and *The Old Ones,* and they have elicited diverse responses from commentators on the later work. Peter Bowering writes approvingly of the way in which "the social predicament" is placed "more firmly in the context of personal suffering and anguish"; Catherine Itzin, from a more radical perspective, is critical of the tendency to deal "either with basically humanist issues . . . or with 'political' subjects in isolation from the overall political system."[17]

Whatever judgment is made on Wesker's change of emphasis, there is general agreement that *The Old Ones* is remarkable for the extent to which the desire to "go deeper into smaller areas" led to the abandonment of "the linear development" of narrative in favor of "a complex patterning of short contrasting scenes."[18] Margery Morgan considers that Wesker succeeded in devising "a more intricate and sophisticated dramatic structure" without forfeiting "the realistic impact" that was one of the strengths of his earlier work.[19] The author himself, wrestling with the formal problems posed by his own definition of the artist's task as "the arrangement of fragments," expressed the fear that he was breaking one of the cardinal rules set down by Aristotle, "creating episodes which do *not* follow one another *inevitably.*"[20] In the finished text, however, the cause-and-effect sequence of chronological plotting is replaced by an equally satisfying order dictated by emotional rhythm and thematic progression. Aesthetic shape and dramatic tension are imposed upon the series of apparently disconnected and disparate episodes—monologues,

lectures, duologues, and ensemble scenes—by the interplay
between a simple forward movement toward a prearranged
social event and the ebb and flow of feeling and argument.

The slight narrative line through the play is supplied by the
preparations for the Jewish festival of Succoth, which begin
in the second scene when Sarah enlists the help of her daughter Rosa and her nephew Martin to build a *Succah*—a symbolic tent partly roofed with branches—on the balcony of her
council flat. In act 1, scene 5, Sarah asks Rudi, another
nephew, to get her some foliage to cover the *Succah;* at the
start of act 2, her brother Boomy joins her in decorating it
with sheaves of dried wheat; two scenes later, Rudi arrives
with a bundle of branches; and in the final scene, almost the
entire cast comes together for the celebratory meal.

The more complex rhythm of the play is established in the
opening scene, when Sarah's other brother, Emanuel or
"Manny," is discovered in his garden in the semidarkness of
a summer dawn, giving vent to a deep-seated sense of deso-
lation: "No light, and no one there. Nothing! . . . There
should be an echo, a coming back or something" (9; 3:133).
This mood is dissipated by the bright sunlight of full morning
and by the approach of his wife with a tray of tea, toast, and
boiled eggs. Manny assumes his daytime stance of dogged
cheerfulness and makes the first sally in a war of quotations
with his younger brother, Boomy, which will continue to the
very end of the play: " 'All things fall and are built again.
And those that build them again are gay' " (10; 3:134). His
antagonist counters these lines of Yeats with a gloomy passage from Carlyle, and it is quickly apparent that the pessimism of the one is a necessary spur to the defiant optimism
of the other: "He keeps me alive, my brother. With his phi-

losophy of doom he keeps me alive'' (12; 3:135). The dispute between Manny and Boomy, who cite Ecclesiastes, Voltaire, Martin Buber, Ruskin, and other sages at regular intervals, is only the most obvious manifestation of a dialectical pattern that is subtly woven into the texture of the play at every level.

Many of the individual scenes have a freestanding quality: Rosa, a careers-advisory officer, tries to instill some sense of purpose and self-esteem into groups of rowdy school-leavers; Teressa, a widowed friend of Sarah's, bravely fights against the loneliness of old age and struggles to translate the unknown poetry of a nineteenth-century Polish woman; Millie, another friend, teeters on the brink of senility; Rudi complains about the world's lack of appreciation for his third-rate paintings; Sarah enjoys the high-spirited nonsense of a cockney neighbor, Jack, and has a tea-party for her friends; Gerda, Manny's wife, is mugged by three young hooligans; Martin is arrested for taking part in a student protest and quarrels with his father, Boomy; Rosa expresses her terror of death and pays a glowing tribute to her mother. In contrast to earlier works, in which thematic issues were often presented in formal discussions among the characters, the contrapuntal technique of *The Old Ones* assembles the evidence but leaves the argument largely unarticulated. It is for members of the audience to engage with the material and make up their own minds.

The characters, many of them based on people in Wesker's own family circle, are vividly brought to life through his keen ear for the speech rhythms of Jewish East Enders; and their monologues, conversations, and disagreements are skillfully juxtaposed to reveal the ''significant patterns'' that he had discerned in this ''very extraordinary collection of tough personalities."[21] The majority of them are old, with ages ranging from "about 68" to "about 72"; the three cousins belong to the next generation—Rudi is "about 40," Rosa "about 32," and Martin "about 28"; and the rising generation is represented by the three anonymous sixteen-year-olds who harass Gerda and the unseen classes of adolescents addressed by Rosa. It is through the complex orchestration of these personalities and their relationships that the play's thematic concerns find expression.

Martin and Rosa are linked by the breakdown of their marriages and by a strong sense of social responsibility; but whereas Rosa struggles to alert her school-leavers to the kind of life that lies ahead of them, Martin has resorted to what Sarah dismisses as the "little gestures" of student violence (59; 3:176). Rudi, in contrast to both of them, is unmarried and is too preoccupied with himself to care about the rest of the world, "I tell you, two things I don't do: I don't jump into other people's business and I don't jump into other people's fights" (25; 3:147). The influences of heredity and environment make themselves felt in contrasting child-parent relationships in the play. Martin quarrels bitterly with Boomy over his broken marriage and his political activities and fears (like Ronnie in the Trilogy) that there is too much of his father in his own makeup: "I look at him and I see myself. That softness? I'll catch it from him and it'll destroy me" (58; 3:176). On the other hand, Rosa rejoices in her rich inheritance from the qualities and example of her mother: "The pompous action that makes me giggle? You! My laughter, my ups, my downs, my patience, my impatience, my love of music, mountains, flowers, knowledge—a reverence for all things living? You! You, you, you!" (57; 3:174–75). Among the older characters, Boomy and Manny embody in their personalities and make explicit in their quotations the pervasive debate about whether one should be "less cheered by goodness than one is tormented by evil." Millie and Teressa are two women who both live alone, one slipping helplessly into forgetfulness and the other talking to herself to keep silence at bay and defiantly refusing to give in to her situation. Gerda finds domestic fulfillment in looking after her husband and his brother but is embittered by her encounter with the three young thugs: "There's a silliness, a—a—nastiness to people which—Ach! Explain to them, tell them things—for what? . . . Hot angers they've got, about grubby little things. So leave me alone about people, all my life I've had people" (67; 3:183). Sarah, on the contrary, will not let negative experiences sour her view of human nature and quickly responds to the slenderest sign of generosity, as her daughter testifies: "I read about the terrible things men do to each other—wars for gain or prestige, massacres for religious principles, cruelty to children, indifference to poverty—and then, one morning, one person, one, does something beautiful and I say, 'See! people *are* good!' You!'' (57; 3:174). Lastly, there is Jack, the one gentile in the cast. In his role as the play's jester, he is very much the warm-hearted East Ender in his affection for Millie and his admiration for Sarah, cracking jokes in dubious taste, ringing his bell, and chanting the wise fool's insight into the inevitability of nature's cycle, "Jack is a-dying, the young folk is living, Jack is a-going, the young folk is coming" (33; 3:154).

In spite of this refrain, however, Wesker has insisted that the play is *not* about dying and coming to terms with death, "Now in *The Old Ones* I was concerned with survival, and to have had the old ones in that play preoccupied with death would somehow not have allowed time to concentrate on how they were surviving."[22] Coming to terms with life rather than death is the crucial issue that lies at the core of this particular work of art. The middle-aged characters of *The Friends* were in the painful process of confronting their personal betrayals and failures; Wesker's "old ones" are the vehicle for a more fundamental interrogation of the nature and value of human existence. For the play's first director, the celebration of a religious festival by a group of secular Jews who had lost touch with their traditions highlighted an important aspect of this central theme: "Growing old is one thing. Growing old without the faith you're supposed to have is another." Wesker denied that this was part of his original conception—"My old ones were concerned about growing old with dignity. Or with fight"—but conceded that the absence of religious faith had become inextricably woven into the play's texture once the Succoth meal had been introduced as the setting for the final scene.[23] With typical forthrightness, Sarah asserts her own humanist belief in response to Rosa's reading aloud of the description of the ancient significance of the symbolic tent, "Let the heavens declare the glory of God, we'll build the 'Succah' to declare the glory of man" (14; 3:137). Nevertheless, the phrases of Rosa's little book sound a base note that resonates through the play, beneath the accumulating evidence of the contrapuntal scenes and the competing interpretations of philosophers, prophets, and theologians flung at each other by Manny and Boomy: " 'The Bible, through the law of the Succah, brings man face to face with the realization of the frailty of human life and the transience of human existence.' . . . 'We cannot measure life quantitatively. It is not the number of years but rather the quality that determines whether life is transient or permanent' '' (14–15; 3:137–38).

That Sarah is the play's chief touchstone of ''quality'' is manifest not only in the moving testimony of her daughter but also in the round of activities that occupies her whenever she is on the stage, drawing a comment from the perceptive Jack: ''You're always doing something, Missus. Cooking, cleaning, watering plants, making us sign petitions. *I* never seen you still'' (34; 3:155). Getting on with the practical business of living with and for other people, as opposed to wallowing in self-indulgent cynicism, also informs Manny's philosophical warfare with his brother. As he settles down to make clothes for children and grandchildren at the end of the first scene, the retired tailor shouts accusingly: ''Boomy! You should work in your old age. Stop thinking so much'' (13; 3:136). At the end of act 1, scene 8, after pouring scorn on Martin's political ideals and lecturing him on his duty to his estranged wife and child, Boomy's parting shot is a verse from Ecclesiastes. Manny's voice is heard at once through the wall, with a quotation aimed at those who presume to preach to others without themselves setting an example to be emulated.

Related to this theme of the quality of human living in general are the more specific issues raised by comparisons between Martin and Rosa as political idealists and between Rudi and Teressa as artists. Martin's justification of violence—''They're leaving us no alternatives'' (59; 3:176)—must be weighed against his cousin's equally desperate but more constructive attempts to combat injustice by opening the minds of her sixteen-year-olds to their vulnerable position in a society only too ready to oppress and exploit them; and while Teressa's verses may be no better than Rudi's pictures, aesthetic value is not the only or chief criterion in judging between the dedication with which she has labored for fifteen years over her translation of the poetry of the unknown Wanda Wilczynski and the competitive and entrepreneurial spirit in which he has approached his latest fad of painting.

The debate between the two brothers necessarily involves questions of a religious nature, an aspect of *The Old Ones* Wesker has played down. Manny, who seeks in the written word some authoritative answer to his bouts of nocturnal depression, will not permit the wanton attack on his wife to destroy his belief in the fundamental goodness of humankind; Boomy triumphantly derides this naive refusal to face the facts: "You know our brother's trouble? He doesn't understand evil. He can't come to terms with the existence of evil. He's always looking for explanations. Some people are colour blind—he's evil blind" (47; 3:166). But Manny is granted his own moment of triumph as the play approaches its close. After squabbling with Gerda and retiring from the party, he rushes back, absurdly wrapped in a towel like a latter-day Archimedes,[24] to proclaim his humanist alternative to the extended diatribe against man's innate selfishness and aggression delivered shortly before by Boomy:

> I got it! I got it! The answer! Listen everybody, I've been thinking and I've been thinking and at last it's come to me. In the bath. . . . Evil! It doesn't exist. It can't. . . . Listen! Evil is when you want to be cruel—right? And cruelty—now listen carefully—[*slowly*] cruelty is when one man is trying to create a situation in which *he* is not suffering pain. (74–75; 3:190–91)

The book Rosa consults in helping her mother to celebrate Succoth focusses attention on another theme that runs through this richly textured play, the need for continuity and respect for the past, so that valuable traditions are not lost but revived in the "minds of new generations" (65; 3:182). This, in turn, connects with the themes of inheritance, social responsibility, and the quality of living that gather to a climax in the last three scenes. Sarah admonishes Martin about the grudge he nurses against his father: "What do you imagine *your* children will say at the sight of such ugliness in protest against ugliness? What must they learn from such a spectacle of your revenge?" (60; 3:177); Rosa makes her most heartfelt and forlorn appeal to her pupils: "Books! Centuries of other people's knowledge, experience. Add it to yours, measure it with yours" (61; 3:179); and Manny finally puts his finger on what is so damaging in the satisfaction that Boomy takes in his constant pronouncements of "doom," "futility," and "life's purposelessness": "No one wants to die, *I* know that; it's a rotten time, old age; just when you're at peace you've got to go. But *that's* a reason to plague youth with our disappointments? We must warn them before they begin that it'll all be for nothing?" (76; 3:192). The argument between the brothers continues unabated to the end, but Manny (like Beatie Bryant before him) finds that he is speaking out at last in his own words, and Boomy's final quotation from Ecclesiastes—"the misery of man is great upon him . . . neither hath he power in the day of death" (78; 3:194)—is spoken against the joyful background of humming, singing, clapping, and laughter that accompanies the delicate Hasidic dance in which Rosa and Sarah express the love that binds them to each other, to their family and friends, and to the traditions of their people.

Glenda Leeming considers that *The Old Ones* and *The Wedding Feast* "stand apart from the mainstream of Wesker's less formally comic writing" because, as comedies, they are "slighter in ambition" and "the brushstrokes of this genre are comparatively simple."[25] Elsewhere, she elaborates the opinion that "the atmosphere of humour" that runs through *The Old Ones* "tends to weight the argument in favour of optimism from the start," and this leads her to question whether there is "any point in pretending to debate the matter at all."[26] Such a view scarcely does justice to the complexity and seriousness of this dramatist's comic art in general and of the finale of *The Old Ones* in particular. It is true that no other play by Wesker closes with the formal comic affirmation of the value and continuity of social life in dance and song. But only in the most facile comedies does the happy celebration of the community's solidarity erase all memory of preceding trials and resolve every problem in anything more than a provisional or temporary sense. This comedy, like the festival of Succoth itself, which supplies its concluding rituals, tempers the holiday mood with a reminder that the "chaos and contradictions" that afflict the optimistic Manny during the hours of darkness cannot be permanently kept at bay. In the second scene, Rosa reads from her little book, "In the season of plenty the Jew rejoices in his prosperity and the rewards of his labours and is inclined to delude himself into thinking that life is secure and durable" (14; 3:137). Not only does Boomy insistently proclaim the transience and helplessness of the individual human creature in counterpoint to Manny's exultant cries of "Me, me, meeeeee!" and the sounds of communal delight, but the bandaged Gerda visibly bears the marks of mindless violence, the absent Martin, unreconciled to his father, is said to be on his way to prison, and Manny's breakthrough to articulateness is a merely personal victory that does not constitute an unassailable refutation of his brother's pessimism. The debate is by no means over.

The Wedding Feast (1974)

The generic status of *The Old Ones* may be open to question, but the dramatist himself has described *The Wedding Feast* as "a formal comedy" and attributed its favorable reception to the fact that "it's very funny, and intellectually undemanding. It has a simple theme which it plays out."[27] It would be a mistake, however, to think that "simple" means "simplistic" or that an "intellectually undemanding" play cannot make serious demands of another kind on an audience. Wesker's most perceptive critics have long recognized that the strength of his drama lies in its emotional power and psychological insight,[28] and he has more than once endorsed this judgment: "I have never written about ideas; rather I've written about people who are animated by ideas. . . . I don't begin with an idea for a play and then invent characters and plot and situation; I begin with experience."[29] As it happens, *The Wedding Feast* is one of only two instances in which Wesker derived the plot and situation from another literary work, although the details of characterization and environment are firmly rooted in first-hand knowledge. It was freely adapted from a short story by Fyodor Dostoevsky entitled "An Unpleasant Predicament," and when Wesker produced the initial draft of the play in February 1972, he was working from a film script that had been laid aside some five years before.[30] The film was to have been set in Italy, but when Wesker returned to the material, it seemed inevitable to make the protagonist Jewish and to transfer the story to the familiar social landscapes of Norfolk, "So again I was using areas from my own experience."[31]

Louis Litvanov is the owner of a shoe factory in Norwich, and is first seen in his country mansion entertaining his manager, his secretary, a local journalist, and the director of a chain of shoe stores. His opening words establish the nature of the comic flaw that will lead to his downfall: "And *why* do you think I make my office of glass? To be *seen* working! . . . I'm a worker. I work hard. . . . My operatives see me work hard. They respect me!" (4:111). As a man who has risen from humble origins—"son of an impoverished Jewish cobbler and grandson of an impoverished Jewish cobbler" (4:113)—he has never lost touch with the political ideals of his youth, when he was "a young communist messenger" (4:115) during the Fascist riots in London in 1936. Unable to reconcile his egalitarian beliefs with the wealth and power that his success within the capitalist system has brought him, Louis lives by what he terms a "simple philosophy," "I love my workers and they love me and because they love me they trust me and because they trust me I can run a factory" (4:113). A series of disappointments, over a bonus scheme, sick pay, an annual Christmas party for his staff, and a sponsored football team—related as a cautionary tale by his secretary and manager—would have convinced a less idealistic or less self-deluded man that the human gulf between employer and employees cannot be bridged by gestures of goodwill. Like Manny, however, he always finds a rational explanation for the greed and selfishness that govern the workers' behavior.

A few evenings later, temporarily stranded by a flat tire, Louis Litvanov hears sounds of merrymaking coming from a nearby cottage and recalls that this is the wedding day of one of his shoe operatives. The incident reminds him of a challenge thrown out during his dinner party—"I mean, supposing you went to their homes. There. Where they live. What then? Would your sense of equality stand up there do you think?" (4:120)—and he decides to seize the opportunity to put his philosophy to the test. He bursts in upon the wedding feast of his dumbfounded workers, and the scene is set for what Wesker's stage directions describe as "*one of the most mortifying episodes in his life*" (4:129). With comic inevitability, Louis blunders from embarrassment to embarrassment until, drunk and dishevelled, he becomes the victim of an innocent game that turns into a vicious demonstration of the workers' resentment against the capitalist. Symbolically beaten with the very shoes that are the symbol of his employees' economic slavery, this well-meaning if sentimental man cannot avoid being cast in the role of exploiter of other men's labor. In the cold light of dawn, he wakes from a drunken slumber, surveys the mess of the party and the wreckage of his own illusions, and shuffles away with the melancholy reflection, "Yes, that's the way it has to be" (4:170).

The rest of the cast, with one or two exceptions, comprises a gallery of one-dimensional comic types. Knocker White, the bridegroom—an accident-prone nonentity, who is already firmly under the thumb of his noisy bride, Daphne Dawson—sinks deeper into despondency as the calamitous events of the evening unfold. His Aunt Emily is a compulsive talker. Mrs. Dawson, his mother-in-law, becomes ever more tight-lipped about the wedding arrangements, and her deaf husband wanders through the play like a ghost, complaining monotonously about the state of the world: "They keep telling me there's an improvement but I can't see it. There's none on it gotten a great deal better. None on it." (4:167). Daphne's sister, Maureen "Skirts" Dawson, flaunts her legs at a bewildered Louis, while Tinker White, on leave from the army, flirts blatantly with his brother's new wife. Daphne's brother, Martin, and his friend, Ringo—the self-appointed wits of the gathering—mock Louis openly and malevolently. Bonky Harris, another of the operatives at the shoe factory, turns up with one of his own amateur paintings as a gift for the newlyweds and stays on to get sublimely drunk. Among those conceived in less broadly comic terms, Stephen Bullock and Kate White are both products of the local grammar school. Stephen is now a reporter and brings the "Lilliputian mentality" of *The Journalists* to bear on Louis's predicament. Kate, elder sister of the bridegroom and Louis's secretary, is the concerned, if frequently exasperated, voice of common sense that tries to prevent Louis from going too far: "Louis, I'm warning you. You're a dear man, but don't depend on my affection to see you safely through social experiments with my family" (4:138). She is "a tired Marxist" (4:114), like so many of Wesker's educated characters, who is as conscious of the "creepy, crawly spites and envies" of her own working-class community as she is of the folly of her boss's attempt to deny the consequences of his economic position. Stephen takes malicious pleasure in summing up her situation: "'Poor

Kate, straddling two worlds. In love with both, and none of you in either, is there, my love?'' (4:145).

The unlikable Stephen occupies the role of narrator in the prologue, which is the one controversial aspect of this play's technique. In four scenes, he introduces the character, the background, and the political philosophy of the protagonist, standing by and commenting while Louis argues his case with his dinner guests, talks with his unsympathetic wife on the telephone, demonstrates his human approach to the workforce in his factory, and comes to his momentous decision to gate-crash the wedding party. Wesker has explained that this method of exposition was designed to liberate the dramatic rhythm of the central action, which is set entirely in the Whites' house, ''To eliminate all that awful plotmaking that so often prevents the process of the play from unfolding.''[32] Glenda Leeming suggests that Stephen's ironic tone was the main source of the reviewers' reservations about the prologue, ''The problem may be that one is never sure how much bias to allow for when he is acting as narrator.''[33] His dismissive style falls into place, however, if it is recognized as a product of the ''Lilliputian mentality'' that labors to diminish the stature of the good and successful. For Stephen displays at the start the self-contempt of a small-minded man who compensates for personal failure by cutting other people down to his own size. In the mouth of such a figure, even words of apparent praise or affirmation take on an edge of derision: ''Louis was an honest man'' (4:122); ''When a good man's determined to do good there ent no stopping him, there ent. Fired by principles he'll defy all scorn'' (4:126); ''And is not cooperation a worthy human aspiration?'' (4:126).

In fact, Wesker cleverly uses his satiric commentator as a device to bring into sharp focus the most testing demand that this "intellectually undemanding" play makes upon its audience, a demand for human sympathy that cuts directly against the grain of what Glenda Leeming defines as "corrective comedy."[34] In the third scene of the prologue, Stephen's patronizing survey of the "conflicts" raging in the breast of "poor Louis Litvanov, husband, father, confused idealist, factory owner," concludes with a challenge across the footlights, "Who would dare pass judgement on a man's actions when such awful conflicts are at work in his soul?" (4:123). He himself later dares to do precisely that, when he sneers at Louis's motives for attempting to meet his employees on human terms: "You came here to court popularity, didn't you? Good ole Liftoff. Just one of the boys" (4:156). But his cynicism is nt allowed to prevail, and there is great pleasure in watching comic judgment meted out when Knocker White, in a rare moment of self-assertion, physically ejects him from the party amid the cheers of the drunken revellers.

There is no doubt that Louis Litvanov commits an act of folly when he intrudes unannounced at the wedding feast, and his folly is compounded by the sentimental vision that drives him on: "I won't be looking for special attention, laurels, flattery, servile humbleness. No! My actions will evoke nobler feelings. Our conversation will be modest, natural, men facing men in a human situation. . . . And when they're old they'll tell their children and I'll be spoken of with affection, honoured, remembered" (4:128–29). There is also no doubt that the genre of "corrective comedy" exists to deflate such self-deluding fantasies. But the satiric perspective on human behavior has no way of coping with a man like Louis, who, for all his stubborn refusal to face facts, is defended by his creator as "warm, attractive": "he not only wants to behave justly but actually does do so. Yet he's caught up in a situation that will inevitably humiliate him."[35] Kate's words over his unconscious body are practical and confront with characteristic honesty the problem that his qualities as a human being pose for "tired Marxists" who long to see the end of an unjust and divisive society: "Perhaps you'll listen to me from now on. Just give them the rate for their work and the sweet, sweet *illusion* that they're equal to any man. Stop pretending it's a reality. [*Pause.*] And don't be kind or ashamed or apologetic for your money. You go around behaving like that, how shall we be able to hit you when the time comes, bor?" (4:168–69). Louis's final speech—"Yes, that's the way it has to be"—indicates that he has at last come to accept the facts of the world he inhabits, but it sounds like a defeat rather than a victory. Perhaps it would have been better if he could have continued to live by the principles his grandfather had instilled into his father long ago in Russia under threat of pogrom: "Take no notice! Don't learn the wrong lessons! That's the way *they* want to behave? Let them! But not you. Honest! Always be honest and peaceful. Don't learn the wrong lessons" (4:113).

Margery Morgan has surely missed the tone of Wesker's treatment of Dostoevsky's story when she writes that "the whip of satire falls equally on him and on the workers who reject his attempt to join in their celebration."[36] As Louis "*wrenches off the blindfold with a profound howl of great rage*" at the climax of the shoe game, he cries out in protest against the ugly passions fostered by the inhuman system he has tried to humanize: "WHAT ARE YOU DOING TO ME?

109

I came here—I wanted to—it was my intention—'' (4:166).
At this moment, he is closer to tragic scapegoat than comic
buffoon, in spite of being subjected to one final pratfall when
he lowers his head wearily into the remains of a plate of
blancmange. Audiences may laugh at the spectacle of folly
corrected, if they will, but Wesker's more generous art dares
them to resist the spirit of mockery, which has already been
dismissed from the stage in the figure of Stephen, and refrain
from passing judgment on this *"huge, tragi-comic clown"*
(4:166).

The Merchant/Shylock (1976)

In his next play, Wesker was to move as close as he has
ever come to a full tragic effect in his reworking of the materials from which Shakespeare fashioned *The Merchant of
Venice*. Although he had always disliked the anti-Semitic
thrust of this somber Elizabethan comedy, it was Jonathan
Miller's 1973 production for the National Theatre that gave
him the original impetus to challenge the familiar portrait of
Shylock, "When Portia suddenly gets to the bit about having
a pound of flesh but no blood, it flashed on me that the kind
of Jew I know would stand up and say, 'Thank god!' ''[37]
Wesker soon realized that any version of the story that
reached its climax with the moneylender uttering these words
would need "to explain how he became involved in such a
bond in the first place,''[38] so he undertook an elaborate program of historical research into the actual circumstances of
the Jews in Venice in the sixteenth century.[39] A world premiere in Stockholm in October 1976 was followed by an ill-
fated American production directed by John Dexter, which

opened at the Plymouth Theater in New York on 16 November 1977, and a British premiere at the Birmingham Repertory Theatre on 12 October 1978.[40]

The Merchant, or *Shylock* as Wesker now prefers to call it,[41] is much more than an adaptation of *The Merchant of Venice.* It is a wholly independent work of art, which draws upon the same sources that Shakespeare used but reconstructs the plot, reconceives the characters, and establishes in accurate detail the economic and political environment that shapes their behavior. Iska Alter has argued, ''Venice, as depicted in *The Merchant,* is an historically specific locale, embedded in a concrete time period of considerable significance—1563 is the year Hebrew publishing is allowed to resume—filled with figures and names from the annals of the Renaissance city.''[42] The term *ghetto,* as Wesker himself has pointed out, is derived from the area just outside Venice known as the New Iron Foundry, or *ghetto nuevo.*[43] Furthermore, Ann-Mari Hedbäck has demonstrated that the Shylock Kolner who dwells within its walls ''is a typical representative of the scholarly loan-banker'' of the period, that the German background and surname Wesker supplies him with are historically appropriate, and that the play's central premise of a friendship between Christian and Jew based on shared intellectual interests ''is a well-documented phenomenon in Renaissance Italy.''[44] Among Wesker's additions to the Shakespearian cast of characters, Solomon Usque, playwright and poet, was a historical person and Rebecca Mendes is modelled on Gracia Nasi, or Mendes, who was instrumental in helping persecuted Jews to escape from Portugal.[45] Indeed, such was the dramatist's concern to validate his reinterpretation of the story of the bond between the Christian merchant

and the Jewish loan-banker that he had to exercise considerable artistic discipline in achieving "the balance between the
documentary material and the plot."[46]

Such a balance was difficult to strike because of the decision to take over most of the main narrative ingredients of the
Shakespearian play and its sources: Antonio's need to borrow
money from Shylock to finance Bassanio's courtship of Portia, the bond, the test of the three caskets, the elopement of
Jessica, the loss of Antonio's ships, the trial before the Doge,
Portia's last-minute intervention, and the confiscation of Shylock's goods.[47] The result is a complexity of plot development unique in Wesker's work. Nevertheless, as an analysis
of the various drafts of the text has revealed, he "insisted on
not letting the story line take precedence over the thematic
material."[48] The first half of the play is largely devoted to
establishing the sociopolitical context, revealing character,
and opening up thematic issues.

Scenes 1 and 3 of act 1 consist of conversations between
Shylock and Antonio.[49] The first contrasts the loan-banker's
boyish enthusiasm for learning, manifested in his collection
of books and manuscripts—"I'm a hoarder of other men's
genius" (4:190)—and the weariness of the Venetian merchant
who is helping him to catalogue them. Antonio's melancholy,
taken over from the opening of Shakespeare's play but remo-
tivated, is a result of the change wrought in him by his
friendship with Shylock: "Those books. Look at them. How
they remind me what I am, what I've done. Nothing! A merchant! A purchaser of this to sell there. A buyer-up and
seller-off. . . . It's such a joyless thing, a bargain. I'm so
weary with trade" (4:191–92). He is like a Beatie Bryant for
whom awakening to the possibilities of personal fulfilment

has come too late in life. Antonio's confession of shame and regret over the wasted years is a foil to the upbeat ending of the second conversation, in which Shylock persuades his friend to ignore the curfew and stay the night in his house: "Stay! You know how the Ghetto is constantly filled with visitors. In the morning Solomon Usque the writer is coming with the daughter of the Portuguese banker Mendes . . . Stay. . . . And if the gatekeepers remember and come looking don't worry, I'll keep them happy. Happy, happy, happy" (4:198). It is from this height of confident prosperity that the play's tragic protagonist will fall.

These two scenes also provide important information about the historical circumstances in which the old men have developed their friendship: the burning of Hebrew books on 12 August 1553, which has caused Shylock to keep his library hidden for the past ten years; the massacres of Jewish communities during the Middle Ages—in Rouen, in London, in York; the segregation of the Jews of Venice in the Ghetto, where the gates are locked each night and whither the Venetian intelligentsia flock during the daytime "to attend the festivals, listen to the music" (4:198). There is also a foreshadowing of later turns of plot in the hint of tension in Shylock's household—his "free and fractious" daughter, Jessica, "cleverer than her illiterate old father" (4:197)—and in Antonio's irritation over the imminent arrival from Milan of his godson, Bassanio, whom he has never met but toward whom he feels some reluctant obligation as the only son of a dear friend of his youth.[50]

The next scene is a demonstration of the quality of life in the Ghetto. It is the next morning, and into the routine bustle and argument of Shylock's family bursts the young architect,

Roderigues da Cunha, eagerly flourishing his plans for a new synagogue. He is closely followed by the visitors from abroad, who bring the latest reports about an outbreak of anti-Jewish persecution in Portugal and enlist Shylock's aid in organizing a financial fund and accommodation for the expected flood of refugees. As Shylock leads one of the newcomers, Rebecca da Mendes, away to inspect his library, the other, Solomon Usque, asks in amazement, "Is that how it is every day?" Tubal, Shylock's business partner, replies, "A house never still," and Antonio expands affectionately on his friend's boundless energy, "When he's not negotiating loans, he's dispatching men around the world to buy him books, or opening the sights of the Ghetto to visiting dignitaries" (4:204). Further insight into Jessica's discontent is provided in a heated discussion with Tubal and Rivka, Shylock's older sister, about her self-taught father's obsession with books and education. She regards him as "an intellectual snob" and resents the way in which he has bullied her with the ideals and passions and dogmas of other men, "My father is full of them and I am oppressed by them and I think my time is done for them" (4:198–99). Tubal's account of the precarious legal situation of the community in the Ghetto sets out the historical circumstances that will motivate Shylock's behavior later in the play, "We survive from contract to contract, not knowing if after five years it will be renewed" (4:205).[51] The latter part of this long scene introduces Bassanio, who tells Antonio about Portia and the test imposed by her father's will—explained as the final eccentricity of an unworldly philosopher—and makes his request for money. In the closing sequence, Shylock persuades Antonio to join him in mockery of a system that forbids brotherhood between a Jew and a Christian: "Barbaric laws? Barbaric bonds! Three thousand ducats against a pound of your flesh" (4:213). The scene ends with Shylock tickling his friend in childish glee, while Jessica and Rivka enter with food and the rest of his family and guests assemble: "*A meal is to be eaten, the sounds and pleasures of hospitality are in the air*" (4:213). The introduction to Shylock in the relative security of his own world is now complete. The rest of act 1 will elaborate on the glimpses that have already been given of the internal and external pressures that threaten that security.

A scene in Antonio's warehouse, mainly devoted to his assistant Graziano's account of his descent from one of the founding families of Venice and a debate between Bassanio and Lorenzo about whether the power of the city lies in trade or moral principle, serves the dual purpose of introducing the plot motif of Lorenzo's love for Jessica and establishing the values of the wider commercial and political society within which the existence of the Jewish minority is grudgingly condoned. Back in the Ghetto, a sitting for a family portrait is disrupted by bitter recriminations between father and daughter, and Solomon Usque issues a warning to Shylock, "You'll drive her into a hasty marriage" (4:222). A dinner party for Shylock in Antonio's house, to which he has invited Bassanio and his two companions, provides the occasion for the various antagonisms of the play to emerge in open conflict— antagonisms between old and young, between Jew and Christian, between intellectual and economic values, between tolerance and fanatical prejudice. The first act concludes with Shylock's exuberant version of the history of Venice, which he locates within the longer and broader history of the upsurge of learning, art, and commerce in the cities of Renaissance Italy. This speech is one of the great dramatic set pieces that Wesker manages so effectively and is to be performed rather than delivered, as the stage directions specify: "*SHYLOCK tells his story with mounting excitement and theatricality, using whatever is around him for props, moving furniture, food, perhaps even people, like men on his chessboard of history*" (4:227). It comes to rest on a characteristic moment of tension and ambivalence. Shylock has just reached a triumphant climax with his joyful image of the rebirth of humane civilization:

> Amazing! Knowledge, like underground springs, fresh and constantly there, till one day—up. Bubbling! For dying men to drink, for survivors from dark and terrible times. I love it! . . . Bubble, bubble, bubble! A little, little lost spring, full of blinding questions and succulent doubts. The word! Unsuspected! Written! Printed! Indestructible! Boom! I love it! (4:229).

He is stopped short by the sound of bells, signalling the time for Jews to return to the Ghetto, and his Christian friend hands him the yellow hat that is the badge of his status as a barely tolerated alien. Shylock "*looks at ANTONIO and shrugs sadly, as though the hat is evidence to refute all he's said.*" But in response to Antonio's helpless question, "What little lost spring can help you now?" he places the hat firmly on his head and goes off chuckling to himself and repeating the words, "Bubble, bubble, bubble!" (4:229).

The exposition of the play's other narrative strand is effected in the second scene of act 1, which introduces Portia, a self-styled "new woman," who "has observed, judged, organized and—crept out of the kitchen" (4:194) and who takes her place in the line of strong, practical women in Wesker's plays, from Sarah Kahn and Beatie Bryant to Kate White and Betty Lemon. When Portia's story is picked up again at the beginning of act 2, the tempo quickens. Bassanio wins Portia's hand by passing the test of the three caskets; Jessica runs away from home and joins Lorenzo; rumors that Antonio's ships have been lost are confirmed; Shylock reels from the double shock of his daughter's flight and the moral situation starkly posed by Rivka—"Who to save—your poor people or your poor friend? . . . And who *will* you save? The one foreign friend you love or the families of your blood you barely know?" (4:239); Shylock's decision that the law must be honored—"I protect my people and my people's contract" (4:242)—is supported by Antonio, who agrees to refuse any explanation of the bond at the trial; a rift opens between Jessica and Lorenzo as she discovers that "his strength is arrogance, his seriousness is pedantry, his devotion is frenzy" (4:247); and Portia determines to appear before the court and offer a legal solution to the legal dilemma.

The pace slows again in the trial scene, to tighten dramatic tension and to allow Antonio an opportunity to make a public declaration of the values by which he now lives and for which he is ready to die. He asserts his commitment to Shylock's creed of knowledge and curiosity against Lorenzo's narrow opinion that "man can be strong and happy with no knowledge, no art" (4:250); and he exposes the hypocrisy of the Venetian attitude toward the financial role of the Jewish loan-bankers: "Usury *must* exist in our city. We have many poor and our economy can't turn without it. . . . Do we condemn

the Jew for doing what our system has *required* him to do?''
(4:253). Shylock, too, is at last goaded into speech by the
patronizing concession that Jews also are human beings: ''After all, has not a Jew eyes? . . . If you prick him, does he not
bleed?'' (4:254). Lorenzo's delivery of these familiar lines—
the one passage that Wesker has taken over from Shakespeare's text—is punctuated by the enraged cries of Shylock,
who finally shouts him down: ''No, no, NO! I will not have
it. . . . I do not want apologies for my humanity. . . . My
humanity is my right, not your bestowed and gracious privilege'' (4:255). Everything is now set for the moment that the
entire play was written to validate: Portia rises, offers her
proof that the contract between the two old friends is not le-
gally binding ''because—impossible,'' and Shylock moves to
embrace Antonio with the words, ''Thank God!'' (4:256).
Portia can offer no help when the Venetian law confiscates
Shylock's goods, however, and elation turns to bitterness as
the old man submits to the power of a system he and Antonio
had tried to subvert with light-hearted mockery: ''No. Take
my books. The law must be observed. We have need of the
law, what need do we have of books?'' (4:258).

The final scene is an epilogue to the tragedy of Shylock,
whose decision to ''make that journey to Jerusalem . . . to be
buried there'' marks the end of his struggle to resist ignorance and bigotry: ''My appetites are dying, dear friend, for
anything in this world. I am so tired of men'' (4:259). A
farewell supper in the garden at Belmont sees the severing of
Jessica's relationship with Lorenzo and Portia's acceptance
that she must make the best of hers with Bassanio. Antonio's
devotion to Portia echoes the theme of the cathedral scenes of
Their Very Own and Golden City, that the failures and disap-

pointments of one generation cannot prevent the rebirth of idealism in the next, "What mixed blessings in these last years of my life: to meet an acerbic old Jew who disturbed my dull complacency, and you, blossoming with purpose, reminding me of a barren life" (4:260). The dialectic between hope and despair is maintained as Portia's words of utopian resolution—"I'll fill my house with poets and philosophers, and politicians who are poets and philosophers. . . . I am to be reckoned with, you know, not merely dutiful" (4:260–61)—give way to the self-satisfied babble of the three young patricians; and the play closes with Portia, Antonio, and Jessica forming *"three lonely points of a triangle which now encircles the grating sounds of an inane conversation"* (4:261).

In Arnold Wesker's estimation, *The Merchant* marks the high point of his achievement as a dramatist. He has spoken of the excitement with which he "discovered the Renaissance" for himself and of his feeling that with the language of this play he had "struck a new vein" in his creativity;[52] and he has reported his conviction "that it is a coming-together of everything I've been trying to do up to now—the nearest I'll ever get to writing a masterpiece."[53] It is certainly a text that distills the essence of much that had exercised him as man and artist over the preceding twenty years; and the objectivity afforded by a historical setting and a ready-made narrative framework lends his restatement of familiar themes something of the representative authority and imaginative power of myth.

Wesker's version of the naturalist preoccupation with heredity and the inescapable influence of the past reappears in Portia's distinction between her father's bequest of ruined estates and the qualities she derives from her mother: "Perhaps that's my real inheritance, Nerissa: father's marriage to a peasant. My energy is hers'' (4:193). Comparison of the two daughters of the play opens up related insights: Jessica rejects the freedom that Shylock believes he is offering her through education, and Portia—Shylock's spiritual heir—embraces liberation through learning but is still bound by her dead father's will. Glenda Leeming suggests that the far from naturalistic story of the three caskets is retained ''as an example and metaphor of the way patriarchal society has the right to dominate even highly educated and intelligent Renaissance women such as Portia (and indeed Jessica).''[54]

Closer to the social realism of the early plays is the careful evocation of an economic and political system that is impervious to the passion of the individual idealist, ''Let us interpret that law as free men, neither Christian nor Jew'' (4:212). Just as Louis Litvanov refused to accept the implications of his role as a capitalist employer and Andrew Cobham chose to ignore the fact that there was no revolutionary situation, so Shylock insists on believing in the inalienable rights of his humanity against all the evidence of racial hatred and persecution. Rivka laments over his tragic blindness as he wrestles with the moral consequences of daring to challenge the prevailing culture:

> Oh Shylock, my young brother. I've watched you, wandering away from Jewish circles, putting your nose out in alien places. I've watched you be restless and pretend you can walk in anybody's streets. . . . But you *can't* pretend you're educated, just as you can't pretend you're not an alien or that this Ghetto has no walls. Pretend, pretend, pretend! All your life! Wanting to be what you're not. Imagining the world as you want. (4:238)

The tragic impetus of act 2 carries him inexorably toward the capitulation to despair that is a greater catastrophe than the material loss of his property and books.

Early on, the debate between optimism and pessimism had been located in Jessica's denial of her father's belief in "Patterns! The scheme of things"—the belief to which he gives exhilarating and flamboyant expression in his lecture on Cassiodorus and the revival of learning. Jessica has much in common with the disillusioned but stubborn Ada of the Trilogy, who resisted her mother's equally stubborn idealism, "Well, I do not believe there is a scheme of things, only chaos and misery, and . . . and in it we must carve out just sufficient order for an ounce of happiness" (4:199). Lorenzo, one of Wesker's rebels, displays a self-righteous iconoclasm that is superficially attractive to Jessica, but she soon sees through him, as Antonio did on first reading his poem, "The Ruin of the Nation's Heart": "Seems it set our youth on fire, full of disgust with the great wretchedness of the world and the sins of men. It had a sense of doom which the poet seemed to enjoy rather more than he was anxious to warn of" (4:210). Shylock's own pursuit of order eventually turns against him, when he is swept up by the tragic process set in motion by his bond, "Seeing what men have done, I know with great weariness the pattern of what they will do, and I have such contempt, such contempt it bewilders me" (4:243). In one of the most painful moments of the play, the contest ritualized in the quotation war between Manny and Boomy becomes an inner conflict that tears Shylock apart: "The balance, dear friend, the balance! Take those books, one by one, place on one side those which record men's terrible deeds, and on the other their magnificence. Deed for deed! Healing beside slaughter, building beside destruction, truth beside lie. (*Pause.*) My contempt, sometimes, knows no bounds. And it has destroyed me'' (4:243). Portia, whose earlier confidence had been couched in a familiar Wesker image—''I could found cities with my strengths, Nerissa, cities undreamed of by any man'' (4:234)—frets under the dead hand of outdated laws at the end of the court scene: ''What should I do? Stand by my yesterdays because *I* have made them? I made today as well! And tomorrow, that I'll make too, and all my days, as my intelligence demands. I was born in a city built upon the Wisdom of Solon, Numa Pompilius, Moses!'' (4:258). Portia speaks for those who know that the social environment that destroyed Shylock is not immutable. Laws, and societies, were made by human beings and may be changed by them. But Shylock himself, the defeated protagonist of Wesker's nearest approach to formal tragedy, surrenders to the negative attitude that denies utopian dreams to future generations, ''You waste your breath, young lady, there was never any such city in the world.''[55]

NOTES

1. See Garry O'Connor, ''Production Casebook No. 2: Arnold Wesker's 'The Friends.' ''

2. See Simon Trussler, Catherine Itzin and Glenda Leeming, ''A Sense of What Should Follow,'' 12.

3. See Wesker, ''A Journal of 'The Journalists.' ''

4. Quoted in Margaret Drabble, ''Profile 10: Arnold Wesker,'' 27.

5. ''Playwriting for the Seventies: Old Theatres, New Audiences, and the Politics of Revolution,'' *Theatre Quarterly* 24 (1976): 68. The *fringe* is the term used to describe the multitude of independent theater groups that sprang up outside the mainstream of commercial theater and the major subsidized companies in the wake of the new political awareness generated by the student demonstrations of 1968.

6. Wesker, *Love Letters on Blue Paper: Three Stories*, 106.

7. Trussler, Itzin and Leeming, "A Sense of What Should Follow," 20.

8. Robert Skloot, "On Playwriting," 39.

9. Catherine Itzin, "A Sense of Dread and Isolation," 9.

10. Wesker, "From a Writer's Notebook," 8.

11. See Wesker, "Casual Condemnations: A Brief Study of the Critic as Censor."

12. Wesker, "Wesker versus Taylor," 23.

13. Wesker, "How to Cope with Criticism," 19. This article is a reply to Harold Hobson's response to an open letter by Wesker entitled "A Cretinue of Critics."

14. Wesker, "A Journal of 'The Journalists,' " 3.

15. Trussler, Itzin and Leeming, "A Sense of What Should Follow," 13.

16. Wesker, "The London Diary for Stockholm," in *Six Sundays in January*, 153.

17. Peter Bowering, "Wesker's Quest for Values," 71; Catherine Itzin, *Stages in the Revolution: Political Theatre in Britain Since 1968*, 112.

18. Bowering, "Wesker's Quest," 70.

19. Margery M. Morgan, "Arnold Wesker: The Celebratory Instinct," 36.

20. Wesker, "From a Writer's Notebook," 11.

21. Trussler, Itzin and Leeming, "A Sense of What Should Follow," 11. In the same interview, Wesker reveals that he overcame "an old-fashioned blockage" by composing an overtly autobiographical text entitled *The New Play*, in which he used the real names of all the characters. *The Old Ones* contains "bits and pieces of dialogue" from this private work (10–11).

22. Ibid., 12.

23. Ronald Hayman, "Arnold Wesker and John Dexter," 94. Wesker records in the same interview that it was in response to Dexter's insistence that the play needed "a framework to contain the whole piece" (93) that he introduced the festival of Succoth into the text.

24. Glenda Leeming notes this "jokey parallel" in *Wesker the Playwright*, 112.

25. Glenda Leeming, "Articulacy and Awareness: The Modulation of Familiar Themes in Wesker's Plays in the Seventies," 65.

26. Leeming, *Wesker the Dramatist*, 114.

27. Trussler, Itzin and Leeming, "A Sense of What Should Follow," 16, 10. In the same interview, Wesker spoke of receiving "the best set of reviews since *Chips with Everything*" for *The Wedding Feast*.

28. Margery Morgan, for example, praises *The Old Ones* as "certainly one of Wesker's finest and potentially most moving plays" ("Arnold

Wesker,'' 37); and Katharine Worth has written of the poignancy that is ''perhaps *the* characteristic note of Wesker's drama'' and of ''its leaning to melancholy and nostalgia'' (*Revolutions in Modern English Drama,* 32–33).

29. Wesker, ''The Nature of Theatre Dialogue,'' 367.

30. See Wesker, ''A Journal of 'The Journalists,' '' 12.

31. Trussler, Itzin and Leeming, ''A Sense of What Should Follow,'' 17.

32. Ibid., 18.

33. Leeming, *Wesker the Playwright,* 122.

34. Ibid., 114.

35. Trussler, Itzin and Leeming, ''A Sense of What Should Follow,'' 18.

36. Morgan, ''Arnold Wesker,'' 33.

37. Trussler, Itzin and Leeming, ''A Sense of What Should Follow,'' 21.

38. Wesker, Preface to *The Merchant* (London: Methuen Student Edition, 1983) liii.

39. In her commentary on *The Merchant* in the Methuen Student Edition cited in the previous note, Glenda Leeming quotes from a diary in which Wesker records the stages of research and composition (xix-xx).

40. Wesker's own account of the New York production can be found in ''Extracts from a New York Journal Kept During Rehearsals of 'The Merchant' 31 July-18 November 1977.'' Wesker records the death of Zero Mostel, who was to play Shylock, after one preview performance in the Forrest Theater, Philadelphia, and the shock of an unfavorable review in the *New York Times,* which killed the production after only four performances, following a triumphant opening night in New York, punctuated ''by applause after applause'' (179).

41. *Shylock* was the title used for a staged reading of the play at the Riverside Studios, Hammersmith, in October 1989, presented in the hope of stimulating interest in a full-scale production in London.

42. Iska Alter, '' 'Barbaric Laws, Barbaric Bonds': Arnold Wesker's *The Merchant,*'' 538.

43. Trussler, Itzin and Leeming, ''A Sense of What Should Follow,'' 22.

44. Ann-Mari Hedbäck, ''The Scheme of Things in Arnold Wesker's *The Merchant,*'' 235–36.

45. Ibid., 236.

46. Ibid., 239. Alter, in '' 'Barbaric Laws, Barbaric Bonds,' '' 547, concludes, from a comparison of the New York promptbook and the published editions (Penguin, 1980, and Methuen, 1983), that: ''From revision to revision, Wesker better integrates his historical material so that the audience does not feel that it is in a classroom rather than a theatre.''

47. He excludes Portia's adoption of a disguise, the business of the rings, and the comic subplot of Lancelot Gobbo and his father.

48. Hedbäck, "The Scheme of Things," 243. Hedbäck's study is based on the six drafts that preceded the first printed text.

49. In the Methuen Student Edition of 1983, Wesker adopted the suggestion of Angela Down, who played Portia in Birmingham, that Portia's solitary scene 2 in act 1 should be moved to become scene 1 of act 2. In the 1990 Penguin edition, in which the play is renamed *Shylock* and which includes revisions made for the workshop production at the Riverside Studios in 1989, he has reverted to the original disposition of scenes.

50. Wesker follows Giovanni Fiorentino's *Il Pecorone* is making Bassanio the godson, not the close friend, of Antonio.

51. In her commentary for the Methuen Student Edition, Glenda Leeming quotes from Mary McCarthy's *Venice Observed* (London: Heinemann, 1961), p. 52: "No Jew, including a native, could stay in Venice without a permit, which cost a considerable sum of money, and which had to be renewed every five, seven, or ten years for an additional fee. . . . The notion that a Jew had rights did not imply any doctrine of equality; the Jew had *specific* rights, the rights he paid to enjoy" (xvi).

52. Skloot, "On Playwriting," 42.

53. Trussler, Itzin and Leeming, "A Sense of What Should Follow," 5.

54. Leeming, *Wesker the Playwright,* 125.

55. This is the reading of the 1980 Penguin text. In the revised texts of 1983 and 1990, Shylock simply shrugs and says, "What can one do?"

CHAPTER FIVE

Solo Voices and the Voice of the People:

Caritas, Annie Wobbler and *Whatever Happened to Betty Lemon?*, and *Beorhtel's Hill*

In his introduction to the fifth volume of his collected plays, *One Woman Plays*, published in 1989, Arnold Wesker was anxious to dispel any suspicion that the series of short dramatic pieces for one actress marked a diminution of his activities as a writer. He pointed out that within five years he had also completed four full-length plays, a ninety-minute radio drama, a libretto for an opera, two one-act plays for schools, and a television adaptation and that he was currently working on a community play "for a cast of hundreds" (5:7). Some of this material was printed the following year in the sixth volume of collected plays, and altogether the fruits of the past decade are a striking confirmation not only of his sustained artistic output but also of another feature of his work to which he had called attention as early as 1969: "No one has acknowledged all my studies of women, or observed how in all the male/female relationships it's the woman who emerges as the strongest and often most sympathetic of the two."[1] From *Caritas, Annie Wobbler* and *Four Portraits—Of Mothers* to *Yardsale, Whatever Happened to Betty Lemon?, When God Wanted a Son, Lady Othello*, and *The Mistress*, the stage plays of the 1980s have focussed upon the experiences and social roles of women of all ages—as mothers, daughters, mistresses, widows, and estranged or abandoned wives. Alongside the often highly individual emphasis of these portraits, the dramatist has continued to explore the problems posed by social structures and the difficulty of reconciling the need for communal justice with the demands of personal freedom.

Caritas (1981)

The last play that Wesker completed in the 1970s, *One More Ride on the Merry-go-round*, was a comic treatment of the themes of responsibility to self and responsibility to society, highlighted by the decision of a professor of philosophy to abandon the work ethic for the travel ethic and to break the professional and domestic chains that bind him to a dead past: "I have not resigned a job and a wife, I've gained my freedom" (6:7). The first play of the next decade confronts some related issues—the distinction between self-sacrifice and self-indulgence, the danger of commitments that imprison rather than liberate the mind—but in a dramatic mode that forms a stark contrast to the preceding comedy of contemporary manners. Like *The Merchant*, it is set in a historically remote period and aspires even more consciously to the quality of myth.

Caritas is based on the story of Christine Carpenter, who lived in the Surrey village of Shere and became an anchoress there—walled up in a cell built onto the side of the church—in 1329. At first sight, this does not appear to be the kind of subject to attract a writer of Wesker's Jewish sympathies and humanist beliefs.[2] The more he researched the fourteenth century and the nature of medieval mysticism, however, the more he felt that valuable insights were to be gained from exposing himself to "a view of the universe I can't accept" and that the bare outline of the historical Christine's life might yield a dramatic experience of archetypal power: "Something in the nature of the act—consisting as it does of retreat, self-sacrifice and suffering—is there in us all."[3] Extracts from a diary reveal that he wrote the first draft of the play between 21 June and 7 July 1980. The earliest printed text, published before it opened at the National Theatre in London on 7 October 1981, differs considerably from the text of the collected edition, which incorporates "substantial changes" made during rehearsals and further revisions "made after the author had worked on the libretto for the opera during the summer of 1988" (6:68).[4]

Wesker admonished himself as he turned from preparatory reading to dramatic composition, "There is so much fascinating history to be resisted."[5] Nevertheless, he decided to set the simple details of Christine's life—her immurement, change of mind, and subsequent madness—against an abortive peasant uprising later in the century. He explains that the two sequences of events, which he dates between July 1377 and July 1381, "are not narratively related but it is hoped that through their juxtaposition the play will make a poetic impact, as a parable does" (6:61). The effect is similar to that in *Chicken Soup with Barley*, with the private drama of the carpenter's daughter unfolding against a background of national and international politics: unpopular taxes levied to finance "wars in France" (34; 6:91); the Peasants' Revolt of 1381 led by Wat Tyler; the growing influence of John Wyclif and the Lollards, whose teachings on "individual con-

science'' (22; 6:77) were subverting the authority of the
Church. The chronological shift into a more politically reso-
nant period is accompanied by a geographical shift from Surrey to Norfolk, which sanctions Wesker's recourse to the
dialect that had served him so well in *Roots* and *The Wedding
Feast*.

Caritas is in two acts, which are constructed on quite different principles but which "must run together" (8; 6:65).
The narrative episodes of act 1 interweave the private experiences of Christine and the public concerns of her village.
An introductory scene enacts the "*ceremony of immurement*"
which, with the smell of incense and the intoning of a Latin
hymn, is designed to saturate the audience "*in an intense religious atmosphere*" (11; 6:69). There is a brief interlude, in
which Christine's parents and Robert Lonle, her former fi-
ancé and her father's apprentice, give vent to their anger and
bewilderment, before the bishop conducts Christine into her
cell and two villagers "*slowly block up the entrance. It is a
chilling sight*" (19; 6:74) This prologue, exploiting the powerful dramatic contrast between the formalized language of
religious ritual and the homely dialect of the Norfolk peasantry, closes with the first sound of the unseen children,
whose repeated chant will punctuate the rest of the play—
tender in this instance, but later turning into a vicious taunt:
"Christ—ine, Christ—ine, had a revelation yet? Had a vision, had a word, had a revelation yet?" (20; 6:75). Later
scenes trace the course of Christine's spiritual journey, as she
attempts to shake off the "old life" that "still clings to her"
(22; 6:77); demands chains and haircloth to mortify her rebellious flesh; prays for a religious sign; undergoes her moment

of revelation, in which she believes she can see "the world's shape" (35; 6:92); recognizes that she has made a mistake—"I do not have the vocation! Release me! I do not have it!" (41;6:99); and is refused permission to break her vow. Act 1 ends with a startling theatrical effect: *"The cell wall revolves slowly. We see the inside of the cell. Backed against the wall is CHRISTINE. The sight of her is shocking. She is dirty, unkempt and terrified as her eyes take in what she now realizes is to be her cell for ever"* (46; 6:104).

Running parallel to Christine's story are the ongoing events of the world of history from which she has withdrawn: the bishop, in his role as administrator of church lands, oversees the punishment of a man who has tried to evade his feudal obligations; a tax collector calls at the carpenter's workshop; a travelling priest preaches the egalitarian doctrines of John Ball—"when Adam delved and Eve span, who was *then* the gentleman?" (41; 6:98); the priest later returns to report the king's meeting with the rebellious peasantry and the riot at Smithfield, which led to the death of Wat Tyler and the execution of John Ball, and to bring home the body of Robert, who had joined the march of the people on London.

The second act, much shorter than act 1, is a single continuous scene in eleven parts, set in the interior of Christine's cell. Wesker has recorded his own reaction at the time of completing the first draft: "Act Two is the strangest piece of writing I've ever committed to paper. It's a collection of moments divided by chants."[6] In performance, these moments *"need to be divided by 'puffs' of light fading in and out with sufficient darkness in between to allow Christine to move into a new framed position"* (8; 6:65). Glenda Leeming comments that the "shape of the play depends totally on the control of the emotion projected by Christine" and notes that in the National Theatre production, "Patti Love's performance, quite intense even in Act One, reached its heights early in Act Two, and the second half became an anatomy of madness rather than a progress towards it."[7] The text indicates a more gradual buildup of dramatic tension, rising through two "moments" in which Christine pleads rationally to God and man for release from her torment to a climactic revelation that comes to her as she is lying on her bed: "There ent one God, there's two. Why would one God make livin' difficult by putting good *and* evil in the world? There *must* be two! Both made the world!" (6:107). These three episodes are separated by glimpses of Christine crouching "*in the corner of her cell, terrified*" and repeating over and over to herself: "I ent narthin', I hev narthin', I desire narthin' save the love of Jesus only." Once, her chant is interrupted by the jeering voices of children and the sight of their hands reaching through the grille that covers the window. In part 7, she is questioned about her vision by the bishop and has sufficient intellectual control left to seize on the charge of heresy as a means of escape: "Not fit, not fit! Let Christine go, she is not fit!" (6:108); and in part 8, she is still desperately trying to preserve her sanity by establishing a daily routine. But the descent into madness is inevitable: in part 9, she is seen cradling a large crucifix in her arms; in part 10, she "*is squeezing one bare breast, part a caress, part a maternal longing*" and intoning a desolate litany of human suffering; and the play reaches its harrowing climax in part 11, as she grabs one of the waving children's hands "*and plunges her teeth into it*" (58; 6:114).

Wesker was clear from the beginning about his approach to the story of the medieval anchoress: "I don't want to enter into the psychology of the act or the girl. . . . The decision, the act itself is so powerful that it carries its own resonance."[8] But he later notes that, given the historical fact of Christine's incarceration, he has "attempted to extract meaning from the experience" (6:61). That meaning is related to his lifelong preoccupation with the plight of those who commit themselves to the pursuit of an ideal. In this play, however, he had found a vehicle for dramatizing the negative effects of commitment to a rigid creed that "kills spontaneous creativity" (6:61) and becomes a prison for the human spirit. Mathew de Redeman, the rector of Christine's local church, sincerely believes that the "solitary life is a search for union with God, it should bring freedom" (6:87). On the other side of the argument, Agnes Carpenter, speaking with the down-to-earth wisdom that animates the Sarahs and Emanuels of Wesker's dramatic universe, recalls how she tried in vain to reason with her daughter: " 'All right,' I say. 'You want to retreat? Retreat! But fastin'? Beatin'? Prayin'? Weave!' I tell her 'Mend the Church's clothes, collect for the poor, minister the sick, comfort the grievin'! But this?' " (6:72). Christine's longing for order is misdirected because it turns its back on other people and the mess they have made of things: "In here's the world. Out there is clutter." Robert counters this justification of her quest for what she later describes as "a oneness time" when "there were oh such peace an' rightness an' a knowing of my place" (26; 6:83) with a question that lays bare the element of escapism in her self-sacrifice: "There's cruelty, p'rhaps, unreason, killin'. But is that God callin' you or man a drivin' you?" (6:79). Robert himself, rather than retreating from the world of men in disgust, will later give his life in the struggle to clear the "clutter" of cruelty and unreason from a society whose guardians, represented by the Bishop of Norwich, also appeal to the principle that sustains Christine's vision: "Order out of chaos! God's Church! To be obeyed! And I will see it is!" (6:77).

Christine's stubborn commitment to her vocation can also be seen as a betrayal of the education that her father took pains to provide for her. Robert's request to "study grammar" is denied by the bishop, who well knows that learning opens the door to free choice—"Us study, us'll leave!" as the carpenter's apprentice succinctly puts it. The intelligent but illiterate artisan bitterly regrets his lost opportunity to thwart an oppressive system: "I must command the word, and if Christine had not retreated to a hole then she'd've been my teacher of the word!" (6:95). Far from being another Beatie Bryant in aspiring to personal illumination, as some reviewers perceived her,[9] Christine Carpenter is a sad example of one whose self-centered pursuit of a dogmatically defined truth has deprived a fellow creature of the key to freedom.

In his introduction to the text, Wesker summed up the cautionary meaning that he found in the story of an obscure and unhappy victim of medieval fanaticism: "The human spirit must be given room to grow, enjoy, to innovate. Anything that suppresses this spirit, whether it is a capitalist or socialist or religious dogma, is anti-human" (6:61). Robert Lonle, the man with whom Christine might have shared both her life and the gift of learning that had been entrusted to her, had once warned her against the willful service of "a private devil" and urged upon her the belief by which he himself lived and for which he died, "God didn't make you for that hole, he made you for the world which he made for you" (6;79). The play's public tragedy lies in the fact that the just cause Robert sought to serve was also betrayed—by those among the people who used the challenge to authority "to pay off ancient scores and murder aliens" (6:103).

With the onset of madness, Christine at last acknowledges the force of Robert's alternative to her mystical glimpse of perfect universal harmony, in which everything "joins and locks and fits and rhymes" (6:92), a fleeting revelation that brought not peace but an immediate revulsion from the grossness of her human imperfections: "Gone. An' I nearly named the parts. (*Pause*.) There's a foul stench in my cell. Arrgh! Who'll rid my cell of its foul stench?" (35–36; 6:92). As she stands with her back to the wall and her legs yearningly apart, she admits "new thoughts which I can't deny. . . . Cos, oh, they're sweet, so sweet":

I'm naked. My body open to the sky, my skin in the grass, sun on my breasts. I feel cool winds bring me the smell of hawthorn and the wild mint. An' I see the birds sweep high an' singin'. An', oh, those clouds, those glorious, rollin' shapes, that sweet scent, that soft air—thaas not the devil's forms, I say. Forgive me, father, but I say thaas never the devil's forms. (58; 6:114)

Her disaster is that this revelation of the beauty and goodness of the world that was made for her comes too late to save her from the life-denying prison that she has allowed her mind to erect around her—a psychological condition by no means unique to the religious culture of the Middle Ages, as is vividly illustrated by the passage about the effects of Maoist ideas on the young in China, which Wesker prints as an epigraph to the text.[10] It is a condition that is given striking emblematic form in the play's final image of the "*poor, mad, imprisoned figure*" feeling her way round the narrow confines of her cell and mumbling to herself: "This is a wall, an' this is a wall, an' this is a wall, an' this is a wall, an' this is a wall, an' this is . . . " (59; 6:115).

Annie Wobbler (1983) and
Whatever Happened to Betty Lemon? (1986)

Christine, in act 2 of *Caritas*, was not the first of Wesker's characters to hold the stage alone in a sustained soliloquy. The "Winter" sequence at the start of *The Four Seasons* consists of a single long speech by Adam directed at an unresponsive or sleeping Beatrice; and Teressa, in *The Old Ones*, has three solo scenes, in which she talks to her own reflection in a mirror, works on the translation of a poem, and tries to convince herself that in spite of being alone she is not lonely. *Annie Wobbler*, however, was the first of his plays to be conceived for one performer, and it was followed by a string of other pieces written on the principles enunciated in the introduction to *One Woman Plays*. Wesker distinguishes there between a monologue, defined as "a person thinking out loud and addressing no one else," and "a play for one actor," which "suggests a person responding to a situation or involved in an action and engaged in an exchange of conflict" (5:7). His own works belong to the second category, since they almost all create circumstances in which "someone else is addressed while an action is taking place" (5:8). For example, Samantha, in *The Mistress*, talks to two tailor's dummies, works on the design of a dress, and goes through her mail, while she waits for a telephone call from her married lover. In the second half of the play, she gets drunk and assumes the voices of the contrasting personalities with which she has endowed the dummies—one sympathetic and indulgent, the other relentless in her interrogation of Samantha's feelings and values. A three-cornered discussion with herself culminates dramatically in the question that Samantha has been evading all evening—"Ask her: How can she *love* a man who betrays his wife?" (5:77)—and a gesture of self-inflicted pain, as she holds her hand on a hot iron to get the accusatory tones of the alter ego she calls "Ninotchka" out of her head.

The origins of *Annie Wobbler*, the first of the three character studies united under that title, go back to 1949, when Wesker was writing "a series of East End sketches." Years later, he sat down to compose Annie's soliloquy as a "homage to a childhood memory" but failed to pursue it beyond the first page. It was not until he became acquainted with the personality and talent of Nichola McAuliffe, who played the bride in the Birmingham production of *The Wedding Feast*, that "those unpredictable writing juices flowed again" and he was able to complete the play.[11] Nichola McAuliffe acted in the English-language premiere at the Birmingham Repertory Theatre on 5 July 1983 under Wesker's own direction, and the play has been seen subsequently in London and New York.

The text is designed for continuous performance, with cleverly contrived costume changes to effect the transition from one character to another: the sixty-year-old Annie, *"part-time tramp, part-time cleaning woman"* in her *"volu-minous skirts"* (5:83); the twenty-five-year-old college grad-uate, Anna, *"over-brimming with energy"* and clad in *"black underwear, suspender belt and black stockings"* (5:91–92); and the forty-one-year-old novelist, Annabella Wharton, elegantly dressed and with her hair in *"a severe bun"* (5:97). Each of these women communes with herself about the nature of her own identity and relation to the world, but each is provided with stage business to engage the visual attention of the theater audience and with a surrogate auditor as a focus for her stream of language. Annie Wobbler scrubs and wipes the floor of a kitchen, prepares and eats a frugal meal, and carefully unpicks the cigarette ends she has collected in the street to restock her tobacco tin; her words are addressed offstage to a nonexistent *"madam"* or to *"a crevice of the far ceiling above the heads of the audience"* where *"God"* appears to reside (5:83). Anna surveys the re-flection in a full-length mirror, which will be the recipient of her questions and observations throughout, and gets herself ready for a dinner date—selecting her shoes, applying her makeup, putting on her dress—until she *"stands tall before the mirror . . . stunning"* (5:97). For Annabella, the same item of stage property becomes a stand-in for the journalist before whom she rehearses her replies to a predictable list of interviewer's questions.

Wesker's 1983 programme note states: "No relationship between these character studies is intended. Each has a life of her own. What I hope will be felt is a poetic relationship."[12] There are certainly parallels and contrasts in the text which generate significances that reach beyond the individual por-traits. The setting of the first in 1939 locates Annie Wobbler's

137

life in an era when there were few employment opportunities for uneducated women from the poorer classes except as domestic servants. Her first position, at the age of seventeen, was in a large house in Surrey, where her young mistress was kind to her but where she stayed for only eighteen months. The pattern of her life from then on has been one of restless drifting, from menial post to menial post—"Don't ask me why, madam. I don't know why. I never knew why" (5:88)— until she is now virtually a vagrant, earning the occasional sixpence for doing household chores for a poor family of Jews in the East End. She has a ready answer to the expected question—"Annie, how did you get like this? . . . Because I was a nothing, madam, and I knowed I was a nothing" (5:87). Having no advantages of person or mind or education—"Got all the parts wrong when they put me together. Needed to rub me out and draw me again"; "I never could read. Nor write. Nor add. Nor dance. Nor talk proper"—she early became resigned to being a "serving-maid-for-other-people"(5:87–88). She admits that most of the time she is "dead or not there"; and she remembers a girl she once worked with—"I used to watch her and get tired"—who was determined to do something with her life: " 'No one's made for service,' she say, 'but you do have to start somewhere, don't you?' "(5:89).

Anna is a reincarnation of this "red-headed steam-engine" from Annie's past, who "filled every second with thinking or asking or doing or planning" (5:89). But born into a later age, she has seized the opportunities offered by education to escape from her working-class background and with her first-class honors degree is confidently poised to take on the chal-

lenges of life: "Against all the cultural odds. (*Calling out*)
You hear that, mother, you old domesday book you? . . . I've
got brains and black underwear and I'm not ashamed!"
(5:94). Her image in the mirror, which she relishes, unlike
Annie, tells her that she is no conventional beauty: "That
trunk surely doesn't belong on those legs. I think I'd better
go back to the shop and get them to sort this lot out, there's
been a terrible mix-up here somewhere"; "I mean *that* is a
face?" (5:92, 95). But nothing can shake her conviction that
"there is a kind of haphazard beauty there" (5:95) and that
the world, in the person of the pompous young intellectual
she is going out to dinner with, is there for her to take by
storm.

The third part of the play is itself divided into three movements, as Annabella, whose fourth novel has brought her
"phenomenal success" and the attentions of the media, tries
out three different personae. The first two are evidently
forced. First, the scatty "mid-culture writer" (5:99), who
deprecates her art—"Nothing *drives* me to write. I just potter
around, you might say. Doodle. Start at the top of the page
and work down" (5:100); second, the forthright, abrasive
competitor, who writes for "Fame, Money, and Power"
(5:104). The third persona seems more natural—tentative,
vulnerable, seeking within herself an honest response to the
questions thrown at her by the imaginary interviewer and ac-
knowledging at the end the dark side of success: "Somewhere within us *all* is a body waiting to give up, don't you
think?" (5:111). It would be too simplistic, however, to re-
gard the third Annabella as the true one and the other two as
false. All three say things that are reminiscent of published

139

remarks by Wesker himself, whose initials his fictional writer shares.[13] Perhaps, like the two dummies who reassure and upset Samantha in *The Mistress*, all three versions of Annabella embody aspects of a single complex personality, just as the voices of Boomy and Manny need not be exclusive but may sound with equal resonance in one mind at different times and in different moods. The third part of *Annie Wobbler*, with its portrayal of a woman no longer safely anonymous like Annie and Anna, dramatizes the painful recognition that the need to project an image of the self for public consumption is part of the price of fame.

Whatever Happened to Betty Lemon? is one of a long line of sympathetic but unsentimental studies of old age that stretches back through the 1970s story, "Said the Old Man to the Young Man," the "collection of tough personalities" in *The Old Ones*, and the Sarah Kahn of act 3 of *Chicken Soup with Barley* to the short story, "Pools," written in 1956.[14] Its title is ambiguous. On the one hand, it implies that the protagonist was formerly in the public eye and has now slipped from view. On the other, it suggests those longer processes of time and environmental influence by which the working-class girl—"Me. Betty Lemon née Rivkind from Dalston Junction," who was once "an athlete!" (5:25, 33)—became the "*old woman crippled by everything old age brings*," widow of Sir James Lemon, Socialist MP for Birmingham North, who is amused by her right to be addressed as "Lady Lemon" and comically astounded at the news that she has been chosen Handicapped Woman of the Year: "Champion Cripple, three cheers! Happy Hobbler of the Year, hurrah! The Season's Paraplegic Princess, pah pom!" (5:25–26). Unlike Sonia in *Love Letters on Blue Paper*, married to another

figure prominent in left-wing politics, Betty Lemon has little
respect or gratitude for her late husband as man or politician:
"Philandering bastard!" (5:25); " 'You play to the gallery,' I
told him, 'Easy solutions and slick slogans. . . . You're filled
with lies and bullshit,' I told him" (5:31). She herself was
never really committed to his world: "Was I ever a socialist?
I *called* myself one in those days because in those days there
was no other name for what I believed" (5:30). Her beliefs—
more an attitude of mind than a set of doctrines—are gradu-
ally assembled in the course of her meditation on the state of
society. They issue in cries of pain and outrage prompted by
the absurdity of the honor that is about to be bestowed upon
her: "What about those handicapped by their impoverished
imaginations, eh?" "And what about those handicapped by
ignorant teachers and bigoted parents?" "And what about
those handicapped by weak minds?" "And what about those
handicapped by demagogues, charlatans, charismatic politicians?" "And what about those handicapped by fear of their
priests?" (5:27, 28, 30, 31, 32).

In spite of the accumulating force of these questions,
Whatever Happened to Betty Lemon? is not merely a vehicle
for some of Wesker's abiding humanist concerns. Above all,
it is a homage to the fortitude, resilience, and sense of fun
that enable a lonely old woman "*to face the day's battles
with obstacles she's determined to overcome*" (5:25). The visual plot traces her physical efforts, with the aid of a walking
frame and a walking stick, to negotiate the task of making
herself a cup of coffee, which involves taking the beans from
the fridge, grinding them, putting them in a filter, and pouring hot water over them. It is evident that her self-respect is
at stake in her resolve to accomplish this complex feat instead

141

of resigning herself to the convenience of an instant brand: "Good coffee. Only the best for the century's cripple" (5:31). And it is typical of Wesker's art and vision that such a mundane chore should be endued with dramatic tension and become a measure of human dignity. Further visual action, much to the consternation of some of the reviewers, is supplied by a recalcitrant electric wheelchair, which teases her by backing away and sidling toward her of its own accord. This is another of those symbolic effects that break the naturalistic mode of Wesker's plays—in this case, objectifying in a grimly comic manner the frustration and humiliation that come with the loss of control over the physical aspects of life: "Why doesn't anything work as I want it to? Not the chair, not my bowels, not my legs, not memory, not brains!"(5:31).

The other symbolic property is the noose of rope that hangs from the ceiling and to which Betty directs her accusing questions. The text describes it as a challenge, "*deliberately erected*" as "*a confrontation with the ultimate*" (5:25). It gains an extra significance when it is used to counter the mood of defeat that threatens to set in toward the end of the play. In her last three questions, Betty turns from the general injustices of society to the personal disappointments and failures of her own life: "What about those handicapped by the wrong relationship until death do them part?" "What about those handicapped by talent, taste, a touch of colour, style?" "And what about those handicapped by despair? What about *them*?" (5:33, 34, 35). She admits that her refusal to be self-effacing—to play the supportive role of politician's wife to Sir James—"kept him out of the Cabinet. My fault. All my fault. Everything my fault. I let 'em win" (5:35) This moment of depression passes when she has the idea of using the rope to lasso the disobedient wheelchair. After much improvised business, she regains control of it and "*circles the space in a kind of triumphant lap of honour*" (5:36). The mood darkens again, as she rehearses her speech as Handicapped Woman of the Year, but even these bleak concluding lines cannot erase the affirmation of her comic triumph over adversity: "My Lords, Ladies and Gentlemen. I wasn't always like this. . . . My Lords, Ladies and Gentlemen . . . I didn't fucking plan it this way" (5:36).

Beorhtel's Hill (1989)

One of the most striking developments in British theater during the 1980s has been the rise of what is known as the Community Play. This kind of drama was pioneered in 1978 by Ann Jellicoe, who wrote and directed a play for the Dorset town of Lyme Regis based on local history and tapping the resources of local people for production and performance. The following year, the Colway Theatre Trust was formed under Ann Jellicoe's directorship with the purpose of making professional expertise available to other communities interested in celebrating the places they lived in. Since then, with the participation of such established dramatists as Howard Barker, David Edgar, and Nick Darke, a growing number of towns have engaged directors, designers, and stage managers from the Trust to help them mount theatrical events.[15] The fortieth anniversary of Basildon in Essex, one of the New Towns designed to cope with the housing shortage after the Second World War, gave Anamaria Wills, director of its newly built Towngate Theatre, an opportunity to launch a similar project. Arnold Wesker was invited to furnish a script, and ·a production team led by John Oram and Steve Woodward was brought in from the Trust.

At first Wesker was reluctant, since he felt that *Their Very Own and Golden City* had exhausted all he had to say on the subject of New Towns and he was not sure that the format of the Community Play suited him.[16] But he was so impressed by the plans for the new theater that he accepted the challenge and on 23 January 1989 appeared before the inhabitants of Basildon to give a public reading of the play he had devised for them. In a preparatory address, he outlined the way in which he had approached the commission:

> I understand my brief to have been the writing of a play inspired by, but not necessarily about, the new town of Basildon, its people and its beginnings, a play which would mark its birth 40 years ago. I was told it could even be a parable about any new town. Not a pageant, not a public relations exercise, not a documentary re-enactment of events but any imaginative assembly of whatever the material confronting me might suggest.[17]

That material consisted of the few published histories of Basildon, manuscripts submitted by people living in and near the town, tape recordings made by the local historical society, and Wesker's own conversations with inhabitants of all ages. Eventually, a dramatic structure began to emerge; ''What slowly took shape as I sat contemplating and sifting the material before me were a series of very strong visual images which could be repeated, like musical themes; a history which threw up issues which echoed again and again through the years; and voices which commented on it all.''[18] The result was *Beorhtel's Hill*, which derived its title from the Saxon name for the ancient village of Basildon and which was performed in the Towngate Theatre by a cast of some 120 men, women, and children between 5 and 17 June 1989.

Among the ''strong visual images'' that lend continuity to the performance and crystallize some of its conflicting moods are the fifteen hooded figures, shrouded in grey, who act as chorus and scene changers; the solitary figure of Brenda, a married woman who sits at her desk and reads extracts from an authentic diary kept by a resident of the town between 1964 and 1968; the group of young children that reappears at various points in the story from 1914 to 1989, growing in numbers and tirelessly chasing the end of the rainbow created by a hologram of lights early in the play; the gangs of rival youths, whose chanting fills the air with the threat of violence; the townspeople rushing to and fro in the rain, ''home to work, work to home, from shopping, to shopping, pushing prams, pushing trolleys,'' while a newly arrived Asian family stands ''beneath their umbrellas, watching, bewildered and lost'' (6);[19] the bunches of red roses, protruding from a plastic shopping bag or held in the hand of a child, which add an incongruous but hopeful touch of color and beauty; the single red rose that provides a symbolic focus for the opening and closing moments of the performance. In addition to these recurring images, there are several of the crowd scenes and visually exciting set pieces that are so typical of Wesker's theater: an evocation of life in the 1920s with everyone ''engaged in a different activity''—preparing food, darning socks, polishing cutlery, playing games, reading comics— ''Living never ceases'' (10); the erection of a prefabricated

bungalow by one of the freeholders from the East End—
known as Plotlanders—who settled on small parcels of land
in the Essex countryside between the wars; a ballet of street
games, which "must be expertly carried out by children who
have been specially selected and who have trained to be spec-
tacular" (21); a stage "crowded with celebrating Londoners"
(29) to mark the end of the Second World War; the replace-
ment of the Plotlanders' makeshift bungalows with huge mod-
els of some of the most recognizable buildings of the New
Town, which "takes shape before our eyes as it is being sung
about" (38).

Accompanying these visual effects are the voices, whose
reminiscences, opinions, and arguments are "shaped and edited" by Wesker's "ear for rhythm" but derived directly
"from what Basildonians have written or uttered."[20] There
are stories about the early settlement by the Plotlanders,
memories of the Second World War, quotations from the
Housing Committee meetings that led to Basildon being des-
ignated a site for development, records of the bitter protests
against the compulsory purchase of Plotlanders' freeholds in
1948, excerpts from speeches by local politicians during a
row over refugees from Uganda in 1972.

Beorhtel's Hill sparked a certain amount of controversy in
the town because, as one national reviewer observed, it is the
"most uncompromisingly individual of community plays."[21]
Wesker's stated aims were to "celebrate without smugness . . . criticise without malevolence . . . disturb but
exhilarate."[22] To this end, he pursued his familiar techniques
of juxtaposing contradictory images and opinions and of
weaving the affirmative and the negative together into a po-

etic texture as complex as that of life itself. Two of the main issues that "echoed again and again" through the particular slice of human life that is the history of Basildon were formulated in the phrases "strangers in their midst" and "the dream versus the reality" (15, 40). As Jill Burrows pointed out, after attending rehearsals, "Basildon has been constantly invaded, not by the oppressor but by the dispossessed." It was this feature of its development from a village of 157 inhabitants in 1881 that the dramatist seized upon: "What appears to have caught Wesker's imagination is how we absorb that which is different from us, how we arrive at understanding our own need to welcome it, even when it appears to be taking our own space and freedoms."[23]

Wesker's chief vehicle for exploring the theme of the stranger is the diary of Brenda. On 5 January 1965, she records feeling "slightly uneasy and depressed" as she contemplates her "new life" in a "new house" in a "new town" (3). Early on, she finds relief from the "neat and clinical" lines of the new estates in "the Link, woodland on one side and a tangle of undergrowth and trees on the other" (5); the death of her mother, left behind when she moved to Basildon, shatters her world "into guilty fragments" (19); and by May 1967, her morale has reached its lowest point, when she writes, "I am beginning to hate this new, self-contained life in this new, self-contained town" (20). She comes to recognize that the quality of living depends largely on personal effort—"I must make friends and learn to fit in here if I am to survive" (26)—and meets the shock of watching bulldozers flatten the woods on the Link with courageous honesty: "I shouldn't mind really, after all I have a house so why do I

147

begrudge others the same opportunity. I shouldn't mind, but I do. How difficult it is to welcome the stranger into your midst, but welcome them we must or die'' (41).

The resilience and moral perceptiveness of Brenda is set against the self-interest of the Plotlanders, who had themselves once been made welcome, when ''they came from London, strangers into the rural midst of villagers who had lived there for centuries'' (19). Their opposition to the plans to develop the New Town—''Strangers will come!'' ''They'll destroy our neighbourhood!'' ''And what will happen to our freeholds?'' (33)—is repeated in the later decision by the elected councillors of this ''town built for the disinherited, the slum dwellers, the bombed out'' (43) to refuse housing to five Asian families during the Ugandan refugee crisis of 1972. Wesker will not let his audience forget this disgraceful betrayal of the dream of a phoenix rising from ''the devastation of war . . . the deprivation of the slums,'' ''Which every citizen could boast / And all the world would marvel at'' (38). In *Their Very Own and Golden City*, Andy Cobham had to fight against the power of big business and the apathy of the trades unions in a attempt to realize his vision. In *Beorhtel's Hill*, the community itself—the ''voice of the people of Basildon''—is raised against ''strangers in their midst'' (44).

Negative attitudes toward ''the people''—''the unthinking, the ill-informed, the pious, the lazy, the illiterate, the easily-incited-led-by-the-nose-flattered-and-fooled majority'' (24)—are focussed in the figure of the Narrator. This ever-present mediator between the play and the audience—an unusual phenomenon in Wesker's drama—admits that he is ''sour and sweet by turns . . . I can be tempted to hope like a virgin, then disappointed like a neglected spinster'' (27). He not only supplies a linking narrative and expresses uneasiness about the values of the Plotlanders—"I'm not sure what I think of your lives!" (12)—he also urges the townsfolk in the auditorium to examine their responses to the celebrated case of a Plotlander who had extorted a large sum from the Development Corporation by standing guard over his house and land with a rifle: "So, we applaud! The hero! The individual who stood up for his rights, defended his castle, got the right price for his property. . . . But thousands were homeless! So, planned town or chaotic development? Beorhtel's Hill or Basildon? And where do *we* stand, dearly beloved?" (37). But the Narrator's skepticism does not go unopposed. His gloomy judgment at the end of act 1—"Most people are just not alive, curious, vivid! It distresses me but it's a fact!"—is called in question by the "glow on the faces of KIDS, the shine in their eyes" and he hands the rose from his buttonhole to one of them as they chase off after the rainbow's end (28).

A third strand of continuous observation, interwoven with the individual testimony of Brenda and the moral commentary of the Narrator is supplied by the chanted verses of the Chorus. This mysterious group, which speaks in a gnomic idiom reminiscent of T. S. Eliot's poetic dramas, opens the play with a dirgelike lament for failing energies: "All things tire of themselves. Youth of its certitude. . . . The rose of its scent. . . . The city of its dreams . . . The sower of his seeds" (2). But toward the end of act 1, there is a change of tone: "Though no joy lasts / No pain lingers / Though the sower flags / The flower blooms / What tires of itself—revives!" (26); and in act 2, the Chorus becomes identified with the vision of a new beginning under the Postwar Labour government: "A health service! Equality for women! Distribution of wealth! Jobs for all! Education for all! New thinking! New towns!" (31). After the Plotlander protests and the rejection of the refugees, it returns to its earlier refrain—"All things tire of themselves. / . . . The rose of its scent. / The city of its dreams" (43)—and it can be seen to represent the impersonal processes of history, which sweep onward in cycles of growth and decay regardless of individual experience and moral concern. The running children, who symbolize the capacity of each generation to renew the dream of a better life, reappear, and the gray-cowled guardians of history form a circle around one of the smallest of tomorrow's citizens: "The last glow of light is upon the runner with a rose held triumphantly high in his hand. The bud opens up into bloom" (46). The very mode of the Community Play is a sign of hope, as Jill Burrows remarks: "Fill the stage with energetic people and that itself is a demonstration of human joy."[24] Wesker's own verdict is that *Beorhtel's Hill* is "perhaps my most optimistic play since *Roots*."[25]

NOTES

1. Wesker, "The London Diary for Stockholm," in *Six Sundays in January*, 162. Wesker elaborates on this topic in "The Women in My Writing: Notes for a Reading," in *Distinctions*, 150–52. Since the publication of *One Woman Plays*, he has completed another play for a singer who is also an actress, entitled *Letter to a Daughter*.

2. Wesker notes that the subject was suggested to him by Paul Levitt, a professor at the University of Colorado (6:65).

3. Extracts from an unpublished diary and notes for the play quoted by Glenda Leeming in *Wesker on File*, 50 and in *Wesker the Playwright*, 142–43.

4. Page references to *Caritas* in the text will be to both the Cape and the Penguin editions where these coincide, but to the Penguin text only when the words come from a revised passage.

5. Quoted in Leeming, ed., *Wesker on File*, 56.

6. Ibid., 57.

7. Leeming, *Wesker the Playwright*, 146.

8. Quoted in Leeming, *Wesker the Playwright*, 142–43.

9. See Leeming, *Wesker the Playwright*, 148–49, for an account of the reviews of the National Theatre production.

10. Wesker quotes from David Bonavia, *The Chinese*, rev. ed. (Harmondsworth: Penguin, 1989), the story of a young woman whose mind was completely dominated by the slogans of the Gang of Four.

11. Wesker gives these details in a 1983 program note reprinted in Leeming, ed., *Wesker on File*, 44.

12. Quoted in Leeming, ed., *Wesker on File*, 44.

13. For example, the "scatty" persona gives an account of her early discovery of Chinese poetry, which is based on a passage in Wesker's contribution to *Bookmarks* (London: Cape, 1975), in which authors were invited by Frederic Raphael to write about books that had influenced them.

14. "Pools" is published in *Six Sundays in January. Whatever Happened to Betty Lemon?* was first performed on 12 November 1986 in Paris. Its London premiere was in a double bill with *Yardsale* on 17 February 1987 at the Lyric Theatre Studio, Hammersmith.

15. For an account of the Community Theatre movement see Ann Jellicoe, *Community Plays: How to Put Them On* (London: Methuen, 1987).

16. See Carol Homden, "Strangers in Their Midst."

17. Extracts from Wesker's address in the Towngate Theatre on 23 January 1989, printed in the program for *Beorhtel's Hill*.

18. Ibid.

19. Page references in the text are to the script of *Beorhtel's Hill* sold at the Towngate Theatre, Basildon.

20. Extract printed in the program. Wesker calculates that 80 percent of the dialogue stems from local oral or written sources.

21. Peter Kemp, *The Independent*, 9 June 1989, 18.

22. Quoted in Homden, "Strangers."

23. Jill Burrows, "Wesker's Angels."

24. Ibid.

25. Quoted in Homden, "Strangers."

CHAPTER SIX

Conclusion:

Restating the Dream

Arnold Wesker's career as a dramatist began with a play that challenged the imaginations of a cosmopolitan group of kitchen workers with "a chance to dream" (55; 2:49). As a lifelong public campaigner, his own dream has always been founded on Sarah Kahn's principles of "love and brotherhood" in *Chicken Soup with Barley* (28; 1:29) and Andy Cobham's declaration of the need "to know, all the time, that change is possible" in *Their Very Own and Golden City* (15; 2:131). When, in the mid 1970s, he was invited to contribute to a collection of essays that reflected "a deep concern for the improvement of the human condition in our time,"[1] Wesker quoted the utopian vision expressed by Andy and his young friends in Durham Cathedral and summed up the priorities that had informed its conception in 1964:

> Priorities based on values that have a long-fought-for and treasured history: socialist, humanist values founded in a society where the means of production are owned in common; where all men earn their living; where privacy and independence are respected in the form of each man's owning his own home; where every man is permitted his imperfection, since that is the nature of humanity; and where material possessions have their value measured by

usefulness, personal association, and the individual's estimation of their beauty. Values based on a love and respect for and belief in art and knowledge. These were fundamentals for me. It was all very clear.[2]

The setbacks of the intervening period had raised disturbing doubts about the validity of his visionary architect's primary item of faith: "In the way you shape a city you shape the habit of a way of life" (63–64; 2:173). What if "the profit motive" were instinctive to man, not merely the product of a materialistic and competitive social system? With the failure of Centre 42 behind him, he found himself wondering: "What do I feel now? Do those same priorities persist?"[3] And in the wider context of the problems addressed by the volume in which his essay appeared, he felt impelled to ask, "With so much of the world underprivileged, dare anyone still maintain pride of place for the teacher and the artist?"[4] His answer, firmly rooted in Andy's belief that "men have minds which some good God has given so we can tackle problems bigger than our daily needs, so we can dream" (63; 2:173), was a resounding affirmation of the centrality of "art and knowledge" in any attempt to give practical realization to a vision of the good life. The city must honor "its teachers and its artists"; "They will keep it free and vibrant and alert to the dangers of tyrants and demagogues and thus fit for the people to live and organize their lives in."[5]

The passing years taught Wesker that the artist's role as guardian of human hopes is a burden as well as a privilege: "Sometimes I resent the dream I've inherited, but then comes a time when I know for certain that the dream must always be restated; with all its naivety and simplicity, its helpless need to believe in man's goodness and reason, its longing for a kind of beauty in his city and nobility in his relationships."[6] And over the years Wesker has never forgotten that his earliest ambition as an artist himself had been to "write about people in a way that will somehow give them an insight to an aspect of life which they may not have had before" and "to impart to them some of the enthusiasm I have for that life."[7] Although he has dwelt time and again on the compromises and betrayals and failing energies that beset the idealists in his plays and stories, he has also celebrated the resilience of those who persist in the face of discouragement and defeat and has devised ways of communicating the occasional victories that can sustain and console the human spirit. On the level of individual experience, there are the representatives of the "intellectually irrepressible free spirit" that lies at the heart of his system of values, a spirit that "implies the supremacy of the human being over the state, over repressive authority, over that which aims to frustrate initiative, cripple imagination, induce conformity."[8] The dying Esther of *The Friends* celebrates it; Beatie Bryant and Simone and Manny break through to it; and, above all, Wesker's Shylock embodies it, "in his friendship, in his passion for books, in his contempt for a racialist law, in the way he reads history."[9] On the level of collective experience, there are those precious occasions when individuals are drawn together as a group by some shared situation or activity into a joyful or comforting sense of their common humanity: the young comrades of the first act of *Chicken Soup with Barley*, animated by their preparations to man the barricades against the Fascists; the conscripts of *Chips with Everything* in the refuge of their "warm hut"; the family and friends united by the Hasidic dance performed by Rosa and Sarah in *The Old Ones*; the Londoners rejoicing in the streets at the end of the Second World War in *Beorhtel's Hill.*

One such moment brings act 2 of *The Wedding Feast* to a magical close. The disastrous meal is in full swing, with Louis Litvanov seated uneasily at the head of the table. He has just aggravated an already embarrassing state of affairs by forcing Bonky Harris, the amateur painter whose canvases have been the focus of some hilarity earlier, into a discussion about his art. The reticent shoe operative mumbles that he just paints the "earth," and the younger guests take up the word and begin singing and shouting it raucously, while Bonky struggles shyly to articulate his vision:

Well. I love earth. That's all. I mean—everything you use in this world comes from the earth. Your own self comes from the earth, don't it? The water you drink comes from the earth. The food you eat in some shape or form, the bricks you use, the tools you use, the wood you use, the match you use, the chairs you sit on, they all come from the earth. [*Pause.*] And when you die—you go back there. Don't you? [*Silence.*] I mean—don't you? (4:163)

"*Then*," says the stage direction, "*at last, the youngsters seem to have found the right note, and a sweet chord rises, as if the table is singing; comes, dies away, to the old ones' 'mms' and 'aahs'.*" This simple happening has remarkable impact in performance, as the voices rise in harmony, overcoming both embarrassment and patronizing laughter. For a moment, barriers of age and class disappear and a fragile bond is established between young and old, between employer and workingmen, and between actors and audience. Such moments cannot last, however, and the mood evaporates when Knocker White clumsily upsets a glass of champagne over Louis. But Wesker's ability to create these kinds of theatrical experiences is as important an aspect of his dramatic art—and as powerful an expression of the "dream" he wishes to communicate—as the verbal formulations that he puts into the mouths of Sarah, Andy, Simone, and Shylock.

Among the many works not discussed in this volume, "The Visit" merits attention as the finest and most substantial of all Wesker's pieces of prose fiction. In it, the author conducts a thoughtful reassessment of his socialist and humanist beliefs in the light of his experiences during the 1970s. The story chronicles the relationships and conversations of two couples during a Whitsun vacation in the Cambridgeshire countryside. The older pair is enjoying a rich and satisfying phase of marriage, and Maddeau in particular, now that her children have grown up, is bursting with confident energy and a renewed appetite for life. During the course of the five-day visit, she intermittently devotes herself to cleaning an enormous brass candlestick covered in the wax of innumerable candles. On the last morning, over a farewell cup of coffee, she gives the candlestick a final polishing: "There it stood, all of them looking at it, the children too, its many bevels throwing off rays of light." Maddeau now faces a decision: "Shall I spray this skin over it to prevent it becoming coated again? Or should it be left, to be rubbed weekly?" The artificial "skin" might keep it from going black for years but would dull "that brilliance at which all were now marvelling" and in which they saw "evidence of energy, pure, reflecting not only the sun's light but a human light." She demonstrates by spraying a small area of the base:

It became at once—mediocre. The answer shone obviously. There was no alternative. It would have to be cleaned again and again, by hand. A family heirloom, to be kept constantly burnished, aglow. No other way. The sparkling surface had to be exposed. There was no protection. Heartbreaking! to have to take all that battering from the elements and then—all that work again. And again. But there it was: no relenting, the old cycle.

And when was it ever not, she thought.[10]

There could be no better symbol for the achievement of a writer for whom art has always been most worthy of itself when it has been in the service of a better life: "So, the dream must be repeated—again and again and again. . . . And though we can't count on it coming in our lifetime (and perhaps, secretly, feel it never will) yet that dream must be lived out here and there, recorded, sung about and left lying about for the young."[11]

NOTES

1. Preface to Dom Moraes, ed., *Voices for Life: Reflections on the Human Condition* (New York: Praeger, 1975) v.

2. Wesker, in *Voices For Life*, 191–92.

3. Ibid., 193.

4. Ibid.

5. Ibid., 196.

6. Wesker, "The London Diary for Stockholm," in *Six Sundays in January*, 186.

7. Wesker, "Let Battle Commence!" 6.

8. Wesker, "The Two Roots of Judaism," 283.

9. Ibid.

10. Wesker, "The Visit," in *Said the Old Man to the Young Man*, 188.

11. Wesker, "The London Diary for Stockholm," 186.

SELECT BIBLIOGRAPHY

Works by Wesker

PUBLISHED PLAYS

Chicken Soup with Barley. In *New English Dramatists*, Vol. 1. Harmondsworth: Penguin, 1959.

Roots. Harmondsworth: Penguin, 1959.

I'm Talking about Jerusalem. Harmondsworth: Penguin, 1960.

The Wesker Trilogy. London: Cape, 1960; New York: Random House, 1961. Contains *Chicken Soup with Barley*, *Roots*, *I'm Talking about Jerusalem*.

The Kitchen In *New English Dramatists*, Vol. 2. Harmondsworth: Penguin, 1960. Rev. ed., London: Cape, 1961; New York, Random House, 1962.

Chips with Everything. London: Cape, 1962; New York, Random House, 1963. Also in *New English Dramatists*, Vol. 7. Harmondsworth: Penguin, 1963.

Menace. In *Jewish Quarterly* 10 (Spring 1963). Revised version in *Six Sundays in January*. London: Cape, 1971.

The Four Seasons. London: Cape, 1966. Also in *New English Dramatists*, Vol. 9. Harmondsworth: Penguin, 1966.

Their Very Own and Golden City. London: Cape, 1966. Also in *New English Dramatists*, Vol. 10. Harmondsworth: Penguin, 1967.

The Friends. London: Cape, 1970.

The Old Ones. In *Plays and Players* 20 (October 1972); London: Cape, 1973. Revised version, London: Blackie, 1974.

The Nottingham Captain. In *Six Sundays in January*. London: Cape, 1974.

The Journalists. London: Writers and Readers Publishing Cooperative, 1975. Also in *The Journalists: A Tryptich* London: Cape, 1979.

The Wedding Feast. In *Plays and Players* 24 (April–May 1977).

The Merchant. East Germany: Henschel Verlag, 1977. Revised version, edited by Glenda Leeming, London: Methuen Student Edition, 1983.

Love Letters on Blue Paper. London: T.Q. Publications with the Writers and Readers Publishing Cooperative, 1978.

Caritas. London: Cape, 1981.

Bluey. In *Words* (August 1985).

Whatever Happened to Betty Lemon? In *Plays International* (April 1987).

Yardsale. In *Plays International* (April 1987).

Four Portraits—Of Mothers. In *Stand* 29 (Winter 1987–88).

Annie Wobbler. In *Words International* (December 1987 and January 1988).

The Mistress. In *Arnold Wesker: Volume 5* Harmondsworth: Penguin, 1989.

Beorhtel's Hill. Basildon: Colway Theatre Trust, 1989.

Little Old Lady. In *New Plays 1*, edited by Peter Terson. Oxford: Oxford University Press, 1988.

Shoe Shine. In *New Plays 3*, edited by Peter Terson. Oxford: Oxford University Press, 1989.

One More Ride on the Merry-go-round. In *Arnold Wesker: Volume 6*. Harmondsworth: Penguin, 1990.

When God Wanted a Son. In *Arnold Wesker: Volume 6*. Harmondsworth: Penguin, 1990.

Lady Othello. In *Arnold Wesker: Volume 6*. Harmondsworth: Penguin, 1990.

COLLECTED EDITIONS

Arnold Wesker: Volume 1. Harmondsworth: Penguin, 1979. Contains *Chicken Soup with Barley*, *Roots*, and *I'm Talking about Jerusalem* (revised version).

Arnold Wesker: Volume 2. Harmondsworth: Penguin, 1990. Contains *The Kitchen*, *The Four Seasons* (revised version), and *Their Very Own and Golden City* (revised version).

Arnold Wesker: Volume 3. Harmondsworth: Penguin, 1990. Contains *Chips with Everything*, *The Friends*, *The Old Ones*, and *Love Letters on Blue Paper*.

Arnold Wesker: Volume 4. Harmondsworth: Penguin, 1990. Contains revised versions of *The Journalists*, *The Wedding Feast*, and *The Merchant* (renamed *Shylock*).

Arnold Wesker: Volume 5. Harmondsworth: Penguin, 1989. Contains *Yardsale*, *Whatever Happened to Betty Lemon?*, *Four Portraits— Of Mothers*, *The Mistress*, and *Annie Wobbler*.

Arnold Wesker: Volume 6. Harmondsworth: Penguin, 1990. Contains *One More Ride on the Merry-go-round*, *Caritas*, *When God Wanted a Son*, *Lady Othello*, and *Bluey*.

The Plays of Arnold Wesker: Volume I. New York: Harper & Row, 1976. Contains *The Kitchen*, *Chicken Soup with Barley*, *Roots*, *I'm Talking about Jerusalem*, and *Chips with Everything*.

The Plays of Arnold Wesker: Volume II. New York: Harper & Row, 1977. Contains *Their Very Own and Golden City*, *The Friends*, and *The Old Ones*.

UNPUBLISHED PLAYS

The following are unpublished and unperformed plays by Wesker.

Information about some of them can be found in Glenda Leeming, *Wesker on File* (London: Methuen, 1985).

"*The New Play*," 1969.

"*Sullied Hands*," 1981.

"*Whitsun*, 1980. Play for television adapted from his short story "The Visit."

"*Breakfast*," Undated. Play for television.

"*Toys*," first draft completed 1985.

"*Letter to a Daughter*," first draft completed August 1990.

SHORT STORY COLLECTIONS

Six Sundays in January. London: Cape, 1971.

Love Letters on Blue Paper: Three Stories. London: Cape, 1974; New York: Harper & Row, 1975.

Say Goodbye: You May Never See Them Again. Scenes from Two East End Backgrounds. Text to accompany paintings by John Allin. London: Cape, 1974.

Said the Old Man to the Young Man. London: Cape, 1978.

Fatlips: A Story for Children. London: Writers and Readers Publishing Cooperative, 1978; New York: Harper & Row, 1978.

Love Letters on Blue Paper and Other Stories. Harmondsworth: Penguin, 1990.

COLLECTIONS OF LECTURES AND ARTICLES

Fears of Fragmentation. London: Cape, 1970.

Words as Definitions of Experience. London: Writers and Readers Publishing Cooperative, 1976.

Journey into Journalism: A Very Personal Account in Four Parts. London: Writers and Readers Publishing Cooperative, 1977.

The Journalists: A Tryptich. London: Cape, 1979.
Distinctions. London: Cape, 1985.

SELECTED INDIVIDUAL ARTICLES

"Let Battle Commence!" *Encore* 5 (September–October 1958). Reprinted in *The Encore Reader*, edited by Charles Marowitz, Tom Milne, and Owen Hale, pp. 96–103. London: Methuen, 1965.

"Discovery." *Transatlantic Review* 5 (1960): 16–18.

"Art Is Not Enough." *The Twentieth Century* 169 (1961): 190–94.

"Art and Action." *The Listener* (10 May 1962): 806–8. Biographical details about East End childhood and account of aims and early days of Centre 42.

"Casual Condemnations: A Brief Study of the Critic as Censor." *Theatre Quarterly* 2 (1971): 16–30.

"From a Writer's Notebook." *Theatre Quarterly* 6 (1972): 8–13.

"A Cretinue of Critics." *Drama* (Winter 1972).

"Wesker versus Taylor." *Plays and Players* 20 (November 1972): 22–25.

"How to Cope with Criticism." *Plays and Players* 20 (December 1972): 18–19.

"The Playwright as Director." *Plays and Players* 21 (February 1974): 10–12.

Contribution to *Voices for Life: Reflections on the Human Condition*, edited by Dom Moraes, pp. 189–205. New York: Praeger, 1975.

"Each One a Landmark." In *Bookmarks*, edited by Frederic Raphael, pp. 154–61. London: Cape, 1975. An account of influence of early reading.

"A Journal of 'The Journalists.' " *Theatre Quarterly* 26 (1977): 3–17.

"Why I Fleshed Out Shylock." *Guardian*, 29 August 1981, 9.

"The Strange Affair of the Actors' Revolt." *Sunday Times*, 30 August 1981, 25–27.

"Debts to the Court." In *At the Royal Court: 25 Years of the English Stage Company*, edited by Richard Findlater, pp. 76–82. Oxford: Amber Lane, 1981.

"Extracts from a New York Journal Kept During Rehearsals of 'The Merchant.' " In *A Night at the Theatre*, edited by Ronald Harwood, pp. 164–81. London: Methuen, 1982.

"The Two Roots of Judaism." Paper written for the Rockefeller Foundation conference in Bellagio, November–December 1982. Printed in *Distinctions*, pp.252–83. London: Cape, 1985.

"So You Want to Write Plays?" *The Observer*, 18 November 1984, 53.

"The Nature of Theatre Dialogue." *New Theatre Quarterly* 8 (1986): 364–68.

"Interpretation: to impose or explain." *Performing Arts Journal* 32 (1988): 62–76.

Secondary Sources

BOOKS ON WESKER

Hayman, Ronald. *Arnold Wesker*. 3d ed. London: Heinemann, 1979. Brief critical introductions to plays up to *Love Letters on Blue Paper*. Also includes two useful interviews with Wesker.

Leeming, Glenda. *Arnold Wesker*. Writers and Their Work Series. London: Longmans, for the British Council, 1972. Brief biographical and critical introduction.

———. *Wesker the Playwright*. London: Methuen, 1983. Most comprehensive study of Wesker's dramatic and nondramatic work up to *Caritas* and *One More Ride on the Merry-go-round*. Includes useful information about productions and reviews.

————, ed. *Wesker on File*. London: Methuen, 1985. Useful compilation of bibliographical material and extracts from reviews, notes and diaries relating to works up to *Annie Wobbler* and *Four Portraits—of Mothers*.

Leeming, Glenda, and Simon Trussler. *The Plays of Arnold Wesker: An Assessment*. London: Gollancz, 1971. Detailed critical treatment of themes and methods in plays up to *The Friends*. Includes a discussion of *Fears of Fragmentation*.

Ribalow, Harold U. *Arnold Wesker*. New York: Twayne, 1965. Places Wesker's work up to *The Four Seasons* in context of British society and the New British Drama.

SELECTED INTERVIEWS

Cleave, Maureen. "If it weren't for the foreigners, I should be in despair." *Observer Magazine*, 4 October 1981, 35–39. Discusses the difficulty of getting his plays performed in London.

Gordon, Giles. "Arnold Wesker: An Interview." *Transatlantic Review* 21 (1966): 15–25. Discusses attitudes to socialism and art in relation to *The Four Seasons, Their Very Own and Golden City*, and Centre 42.

Hayman, Ronald. *Arnold Wesker*. 3d. ed. London: Heinemann, 1979, pp. 1–12 and 92–102. Two valuable interviews in which Wesker discusses the autobiographical element in his work and the origins of Centre 42 and responds to criticism of his plays.

————. "Arnold Wesker and John Dexter." *Transatlantic Review* 48 (1973–74): 89–99. Conversation about the working relationship between Wesker and the director of his early plays.

"An Interview with Arnold Wesker: Centre 42." *Encore* 9 (May–June 1962): 39–44.

Kitchin, Laurence. "Playwright to Watch." *Times*, 21 September 1959: 5. Reprinted in *Mid-Century Drama*. 2d ed., pp. 194–96. London: Faber & Faber, 1962. Contains biographical information.

Skloot, Robert. "On Playwriting: Interview with Arnold Wesker." *Performing Arts Journal* 2 (1978): 38–47. Discusses the Jewish element in the plays and Wesker's changing attitudes to socialism.

Stoll, Karl-Heinz. "Interviews with Edward Bond and Arnold Wesker." *Twentieth-Century Literature* 22 (1976): 422–32. Discusses productions of *The Kitchen* and *The Wedding Feast* in East Germany and his methods of working.

"The System and the Writer: Wesker Interviewed." *New Theatre Magazine* 11 (1971): 8–11. Discusses staging of early plays and the role of art in society.

Trussler, Simon. "His Very Own and Golden City." *Tulane Drama Review* 11 (1966–67): 192–202. Reprinted in *Theatre at Work: Playwrights and Productions in the Modern British Theatre*, edited by Charles Marowitz and Simon Trussler, pp. 78–95. New York: Hill and Wang, 1967. Discusses relation between life and work, Centre 42, the nature of dramatic dialogue, the composition of *Their Very Own and Golden City* and *The Four Seasons*.

Trussler, Simon, Catherine Itzin, and Glenda Leeming. "A Sense of What Should Follow." *Theatre Quarterly* 28 (1977): 5–24. A review of Wesker's career, with special attention to the writing and staging of later plays from *The Friends* to *The Merchant*.

Wager, Walter. "Interview with Arnold Wesker." *Playbill* (1964). Reprinted in *The Playwrights Speak*, edited by Walter Wager, pp. 213–30. London: Longmans, 1969. Discusses working methods and Centre 42.

Wolf, Matt. "From Merchant to Shylock." *City Limits*, 12–19 October 1989: 68. Discusses *The Merchant* and its Shakespearian source.

SELECTED ARTICLES AND CHAPTERS IN BOOKS ON WESKER

Adler, Thomas P. "*The Wesker Trilogy* Revisited: Games to Compensate for the Inadequacy of Words." *The Quarterly Journal of Speech* 65 (1979): 429–38. Sees the games and rituals in the plays as a means of liberating author and audience from sole dependence on language to communicate feelings and significances.

Alter, Iska. " 'Barbaric Laws, Barbaric Bonds': Arnold Wesker's *The Merchant.*" *Modern Drama* 31 (1988): 536–47. Discusses changes of emphasis in Wesker's reworking of the Shakespearian material in the light of historical research.

Anderson, Michael. "Arnold Wesker: The Last Humanist?" *New Theatre Magazine* 8 (1968): 10–27. Sees Wesker's work up to *Their Very Own and Golden City* as expressive of passionate belief in man. Detailed analysis of the early plays demonstrates the combination of unsentimental idealism and realism in his social vision.

Appignanesi, Richard. "Finding One's Own Voice: An Afterword on Wesker's WORDS and His Plays." In *Words as Definitions of Experience*, by Arnold Wesker, afterword. London: Writers and Readers Publishing Cooperative, 1976. Discusses the relation between Wesker's concern for language and his "rational vision."

Bowering, Peter. "Wesker's Quest for Values." *Adam: International Review* 401–3 (1977–78): 69–85. Discusses Wesker's move toward a less overtly didactic drama, striking a balance between personal and social themes, in *The Friends*, *The Old Ones*, and *Love Letters on Blue Paper*.

Brown, John Russell. *Theatre Language: A Study of Arden, Osborne, Pinter and Wesker*. London: Allen Lane, 1972. Chapter on dramatic techniques in plays from *The Kitchen* to *The Friends*.

Burrows, Jill. "Wesker's Angels." *Times Educational Supplement* 26 May 1989; B5. Describes rehearsals of *Beorhtel's Hill*.

Chambers, Colin, and Mike Prior. *Playwrights' Progress: Patterns of Postwar British Drama*. Oxford: Amber Lane, 1987. Chapter on the morally defined socialism of The Trilogy.

Coppieters, Frank. "Arnold Wesker's Centre Fortytwo: A Cultural Revolution Betrayed." *Theatre Quarterly* 18 (1975): 37–54. Detailed account of the rise and fall of the Centre 42 project.

Costello, Tom. "The Defeat of Naturalism in Arnold Wesker's *Roots*." *Modern Drama* 21 (1978): 39–46. Discusses romantic and mythopoetic elements that subvert the surface naturalism of *Roots*.

Dexter, John. "Working with Arnold." *Plays and Players* 9 (April 1962): 11. Describes the collaboration between Wesker, Dexter, and designer Jocelyn Herbert on productions of early plays.

———. "Chips and Devotion." *Plays and Players* 10 (December 1962): 32. Director discusses rehearsals of *Chips with Everything*.

Drabble, Margaret. "Profile 10: Arnold Wesker." *New Review* 11 (1975): 25–30. Discusses Wesker's neglect in Britain and his habit of fighting back. Includes a brief account of the short stories.

Findlater, Richard. "Plays and Politics." *The Twentieth Century* 168 (1960): 235–42. Argues that the promise of the Trilogy lies not in its political thinking, which is confused and shallow, but in its burning moral concern and emotional power.

Garforth, John. "Arnold Wesker's Mission." *Encore* 10 (May–June 1963): Reprinted in *The Encore Reader*, edited by Charles Marowtiz, Tom Milne, and Owen Hale, pp. 223–30. London: Methuen, 1965. Argues that Wesker's social message is confused and based on a mistaken view of working-class culture shared by many well-intentioned liberal idealists.

Goodman, Henry. "The New Dramatists: 2. Arnold Wesker." *Drama Survey* 1 (1961): 215–22. Compares the old-style realism and political commitment of Wesker's early plays to the work of Clifford Odets.

Hedbäck, Ann-Mari. "The Scheme of Things in Arnold Wesker's *The Merchant*." *Studia Neophilologica* 51 (1979): 233–44. An account of the historical accuracy of the Venetian world of Wesker's play and of revisions to various drafts of the text.

Homden, Carol. "Strangers in Their Midst." *Art East* (June 1989). An account of Wesker's involvement with the Basildon community during the writing and production of *Beorhtel's Hill*.

Itzin, Catherine. "A Sense of Dread and Isolation." *Tribune*, 13 October 1978: 8–9. An account of the setbacks to Wesker's career in the 1970s and of his growing sense of political impotence.

————. *Stages in the Revolution: Political Theatre in Britain Since 1968*, pp. 102–15. London: Eyre Methuen, 1980. Discusses Wesker's alienation from the Left during the 1970s and documents his dispute about politics and drama with John McGrath.

Jones, A. R. "The Theatre of Arnold Wesker." *Critical Quarterly* 2 (1960): 366–70. Positive critical response to the Trilogy.

Kershaw, John. *The Present Stage: New Directions in the Theatre Today*, pp. 43–53. London: Collins, 1966. Chapter on *Roots*.

Kitchin, Laurence. *Mid-Century Drama*. 2d ed., pp. 112–14. London: Faber, 1962. Discusses *Roots* as a masterpiece of the new drama.

————. "Drama with a Message: Arnold Wesker." In *Experimental Drama*, edited by William A. Armstrong, pp. 169–85. London: Bell, 1963. Contains an analysis of *The Kitchen* and an appraisal of Wesker's early achievements.

Kustow, Michael. "Wesker at the Half-way House." *Plays and Players* 21 (October 1973): 32–35. Positive reassessment of Wesker's work in the late 1960s and early 1970s and of the construction of the plays.

Latham, Jacqueline. "*Roots*: A Reassessment." *Modern Drama* 8 (1965): 192–97. Discusses the language of the play and the element of irony which complicates the play's attitude towards the Bryants.

Leech, Clifford. "Two Romantics: Arnold Wesker and Harold Pinter." In *Contemporary Theatre*, edited by John Russell Brown and Bernard Harris, pp. 10–31. Stratford-upon-Avon Studies 4. London: Arnold, 1962. Discusses *The Kitchen* and the Trilogy as realist plays.

Leeming, Glenda. "Articulacy and Awareness: The Modulation of Familiar Themes in Wesker's Plays of the 70s." In *Contemporary English Drama*, edited by C. W. E. Bigsby, pp. 64-77. Stratford-upon-Avon Studies 19. London: Arnold, 1981. Sees *The Old Ones* and *The Wedding Feast* as comedies and *The Friends*, *The Journalists*, and *The Merchant* as representing a steady advance toward the integration of individual suffering with more public concerns.

Lloyd Evans, Gareth. *The Language of Modern Drama*, pp. 87–102. London: Dent, 1977. Charts Wesker's move away from the authentic-sounding speech of the underprivileged in the Trilogy to a more private and stylized idiom in works of the 1960s.

Mander, John. *The Writer and Commitment*, pp. 194–210. London: Secker & Warburg, 1961. A discussion of the dialectical method of *Roots*.

Mannheimer, Monica. "Major Themes in Arnold Wesker's Play *The Friends*." *Moderna Språk* 66 (1972): 109–16. Examines themes of order and chaos, isolation and communication, and the social responsibility of the artist.

———. "Ordering Chaos: The Genesis of Arnold Wesker's *The Friends*." *English Studies* 56 (1975): 34–44. Analysis of the development of the play through six drafts to a final version.

Morgan, Margery M. "Arnold Wesker: The Celebratory Instinct." In *Essays on Contemporary British Drama*, edited by Hedwig Bock and Albert Werthweim, pp. 31–45. Munchen: Max Hueber Verlag, 1981. A survey of Wesker's work that locates its greatest strength in its controlled and conflicting emotion.

Mutalik-Desai, A. A. "*The Wesker Trilogy*: Propaganda or Allegory?" *Indian Journal of English Studies* 26 (1987): 5–13.

O'Connor, Garry. "Production Casebook No. 2: Arnold Wesker's 'The Friends.' " *Theatre Quarterly* 2 (1971): 78–92. An account of rehearsals of the 1970 Round House production directed by Wesker.

Orr, John. *Tragic Drama and Modern Society: A Sociology of Dramatic Form from 1880 to the Present* 2d ed., pp. 262–65. Basingstoke: Macmillan, 1989. Sees the Trilogy as an important breakthrough in the dramatic presentation of working-class experience.

Page, Malcolm. "Whatever Happened to Arnold Wesker?: His Recent Plays." *Modern Drama* 11 (1968): 317–25. Discusses *Chips with Everything*, *The Four Seasons*, and *Their Very Own and Golden City*.

Rabey, David Ian. *British and Irish Political Drama in the Twentieth Century*, pp. 84–88. Basingstoke: Macmillan, 1986. Sees Wesker's socialism as humanistic rather than ideological.

Scott, Michael. *Shakespeare and the Modern Dramatist*, pp. 44–59. Basingstoke: Macmillan, 1989. Places Wesker's objections to the anti-Semitism of Shakespeare's *The Merchant of Venice* in the context of stage traditions and discusses the methods used to demythologize the figure of Shylock in *The Merchant*.

Sinfield, Alan. "Making Space: Appropriation and Confrontation in Recent British Plays." In *The Shakespeare Myth*, edited by Graham Holderness, pp. 128–44. Manchester: Manchester University Press, 1988. Includes a brief and unsympathetic section on Wesker's *The Merchant*.

Stevens, Mary. "Wesker's The Wesker Trilogy." *The Explicator* 43: 3 (1985): 45–48. Discusses implications of Ronnie's story of the girl, the two lovers, and the wiseman in *Roots*.

Taylor, John Russell. *Anger and After: A Guide to the New British Drama*, pp. 147–70. 2d ed. London: Methuen, 1969. Questions both the authenticity of the portraits of working-class life and the control of dramatic structure in the early plays.

Tynan, Kenneth. *A View of the English Stage*, pp. 289–99. St. Albans: Paladin, 1976. Reviews of Royal Court production of the Trilogy in 1960.

Wandor, Michelene. *Look Back in Gender: Sexuality and the Family in Post-War British Drama*. London: Methuen, 1987. Chapter on the Trilogy.

Wellwarth, George E. *The Theatre of Protest and Paradox: Developments in the Avant-Garde Drama*, pp. 234–43. London: MacGibbon & Kee, 1965. Sees Wesker's attempts to portray life of ordinary people as caricature derived from stock literary materials.

Worth, Katharine J. *Revolutions in Modern English Drama*, pp. 30–38. London: Bell, 1972. Discusses tension between naturalism and expressionism and emphasises the element of poignant clowning.

Zimmermann, Heinz. "Wesker and Utopia in the Sixties." *Modern Drama* 29 (1986): 185–206. Discusses Messianic and nineteenth-century roots of the utopian socialism of the plays from *The Kitchen* to *The Friends*.

Index